NEW ZEALAND THROUGH TIME

RONALD COMETTI

NEW ZEALAND THROUGH TIME

An illustrated journey through 83 million years of natural history

NEW
HOLLAND

This book is dedicated to my wife, Ronella.

We think in terms of eternity,
But we move slowly through time.

from 'Towards the Beautiful Gate'
by Oscar Wilde

First published in 2008 by New Holland Publishers (NZ) Ltd
Auckland • Sydney • London • Cape Town

www.newhollandpublishers.co.nz

218 Lake Road, Northcote, Auckland 0627, New Zealand
Unit 1, 66 Gibbes Street, Chatswood, NSW 2067, Australia
86–88 Edgware Road, London W2 2EA, United Kingdom
80 McKenzie Street, Cape Town 8001, South Africa

Publishing manager/editorial direction: Matt Turner
Design: Dexter Fry
Maps: Nick Keenleyside
Consultants: Brian Gill, Hamish Campbell, Ronald Keam

National Library of New Zealand Cataloguing-in-Publication Data

Cometti, Ronald.
New Zealand through time : an illustrated journey through 83
million years of natural history / Ronald Cometti.
Includes bibliographical references and index.
ISBN 978-1-86966-163-2
1. Natural history—New Zealand. I. Title.
508.93—dc 22

10 9 8 7 6 5 4 3 2 1

Colour reproduction by SC (Sang Choy) International Pte Ltd,
Singapore, and Image Centre Ltd, New Zealand.
Printed by SNP Leefung in China, on paper sourced from
sustainable forests.

Contents

PREFACE

In geological terms, New Zealand is relatively young and highly unstable, with rocks that range in age from over half a billion years old to brand-new. This chain of islands amid the Pacific is perhaps better thought of as the emergent part of a giant sunken continent, to which geologists refer as Zealandia.

New Zealand Through Time traces the progress of Zealandia from the point 83 million years ago when, under the power of colossal tectonic forces, it rifted from the great southern supercontinent Gondwana and drifted out alone across the ocean. The book brings us almost up to date with an account of the 1931 earthquake that struck the Hawke's Bay region – just one of many geological upheavals that have wrought tremendous, and sometimes catastrophic, changes to the landscape as well as the land's shape during New Zealand's long journey through time. These upheavals have especially affected our fauna, which has evolved in tandem with changes in temperature, weather patterns and sea levels. Much of New Zealand's native flora evolved on Gondwana and has changed so little that walking into our native forests is like stepping back more than 80 million years in time. Changes to our native fauna, however, have been more dramatic. As this book will show, at first the land was ruled by dinosaurs – live cargo from Gondwana – and our seas were dominated by huge marine reptiles, alongside innumerable fish and marine invertebrates.

After the dinosaurs died out 65 million years ago, Zealandia's wildlife took on a radically different character from that which occupied land masses elsewhere in the world. With almost no land mammals to speak of, a host of other creatures held sway – we once had quite a large crocodile – and until the arrival of Polynesian explorers over seven centuries ago, New Zealand had become 'the land that time forgot'. Within the forests and along the shores dwelt an amazing variety of primitive reptiles, insects, frogs, and flightless or near flightless birds.

After those first Polynesian explorers arrived and made themselves at home, human-made changes to the natural ecosystem began in earnest, increasing rapidly after Europeans came to these islands and named them New Zealand (Aotearoa is only a recent name). Extinctions of our native fauna and flora have been rapid, numerous and lamentable. Chapter by chapter, this book looks at the significant episodes that have punctuated our time-travelling history.

As an author and illustrator who has dedicated most of his life to painting, illustrating, and learning and writing about New Zealand's natural history, my experiences in the field have provided me with good grounding. These have included more than two decades' work as a natural history tour leader, teaching and leading thousands of overseas tourists through this land, and also as a guest lecturer on visiting cruise ships. My travels have taken me from North Cape down to magical Stewart Island, and twice to our superb subantarctic islands.

Now, as I end my working career, I realise that this book is not only a testament to all that I have seen and studied, it is also a plea for others to continue this work in the hope it may eventually lead to the establishment of a natural history museum, one to equal any the world over: a showcase for our living and extinct treasures from the subtropical north down to Antarctica, both in the sea and on the land. As we head out through the twenty-first century, a 'New Zealand Museum of Natural History' is not just a dream that many scientists and conservationists have; it has become essential in order that people, especially children from this and other lands, may also learn and marvel at our unique, fascinating and extraordinary natural history – highlighted, illustrated and written about in *New Zealand Through Time*.

Acknowledgements

I WOULD LIKE TO EXPRESS my gratitude to friends and family for their help and support during the creation of this book. My thanks go out in particular to Brian Gill of the Auckland War Memorial Museum for reading the text, and also to Hamish Campbell and Ronald Keam for their assistance as consultants.

Ronald Cometti
Orewa

Measuring the Earth's Age

Tracing the planet's history – finding out when mountains arose, sea levels rose or fell, the various plants and animals evolved or died out, and so forth – is a process of studying changes that took place very slowly. This is generally achieved by analysing rocks and fossils. And although the techniques for analysis have advanced with modern science, the basic dating system to which geologists – and this book – constantly refer is the *geologic time scale*.

A brief history of the time scale

The time scale is being updated all the time, but its roots go back centuries. Leonardo da Vinci in the sixteenth century and Danish geologist Nicolaus Steno (in the seventeenth) had both proposed that the Earth's rocks were laid down in layers, one after the other, over long periods of time. This may seems obvious to us now; but in their day the Church's view prevailed, which is to say that the Earth had been created in six days and was now 6000–7000 years old (a figure reached by adding up all the post-Adam generations listed in the Bible).

Gradually, geologists created a scientific system for *relative dating*: that is, establishing whether one rock layer, together with the fossils embedded within it, was older or younger than another. There were many complex issues to

Below: A simplified geological time scale, with dates in millions of years. The pre-Cambrian era, covering the first 4 billion years, is compressed into a small space for convenience, since very little complex life flourished during this long period of time. A fully detailed version of the time scale created for the geology of New Zealand is published by GNS in Wellington (www.gns.cri.govt.nz).

		The first invertebrates		The first fishes			Horsetails and clubmosses			318	Reptiles appear
							Sharks		Mississippian		Pennsylvanian
Era	Period	Epoch									
		4600		542	490	443	417	359		299	
		Precambrian	Cambrian		Ordovician	Silurian	Devonian	Carboniferous			Permian
					PALEOZOIC						

resolve. It became evident, for example, that rocks laid down at the same time in different parts of the world could look very different from one another, and furthermore could later be dramatically altered by the planet's dynamic forces, such as the movement of tectonic plates (see Chapter 1).

At the turn of the twentieth century, the discovery of radioactivity provided a means of *absolute dating*: that is, calculating the age (in years) of a rock, mineral or fossil. This is achieved by studying the decay rates of unstable elements such as carbon, lead and uranium. Rather surprisingly for the Church, scientists could now state with confidence that the Earth was around 4.6 billion years old.

How it works

The geological time scale connects relative dates with absolute dates: it plots geological events against a real time scale that is calibrated in thousands, millions and billions of years. The scale is also divided into units of time, called (from largest to smallest) eons, eras, periods and epochs. The units are named after localities containing rocks of the age they describe. For example, the Jurassic period was named after the Jura Mountains on the Swiss-French border. The boundary between one unit and the next usually corresponds to a major event, such as a mass extinction. For instance, the mass extinction of dinosaurs and marine reptiles 65 million years ago marks the end of the Cretaceous period; and the following period, the Paleogene, sees the rise of the mammals. In this way, the units mark out the ages of the Earth: its history.

You may find it convenient to bookmark these pages, since the book makes constant references to the various units of the time scale.

				PALEOCENE	EOCENE 55.5	OLIGOCENE 33.7	MIOCENE	PLIOCENE 5.3 / PLEISTOCENE 1.8
rly mammals		*Evolution and rapid spread of flowering plants*						
Rise of the dinosaurs			*83 mya: Zealandia separates from Gondwana*					
TRIASSIC 200	JURASSIC 146		CRETACEOUS 65	PALEOGENE		24	NEOGENE	
MESOZOIC				*CENOZOIC*				

Chapter 1

The Long Isolation Begins

83 million years ago

In a humid bush clearing on the Chatham Rise several hundred kilometres to the east of what is now New Zealand, an ankylosaur moves slowly among a lush patch of buttercups, a favoured food plant. From tail tip to bony snout the dinosaur measures a little under 2 metres long, and all along the upper parts of its low, rounded body a covering of bony plates and spines gives it almost complete protection from predators.

Nearby, a herd of light-footed hypsilophodontids grazes cautiously, staying alert to danger. A crashing of undergrowth causes them all to look up as one: a 10-metre-long allosaurid bounds towards them. Startled, they flee, massing into one flowing group as they streak for the safety of nearby tree ferns and cycads, and as they melt from sight the allosaurid's gaze swivels to the ankylosaur.

The ankylosaur, too, has sensed the threat. A heavy plant-eater, it has no hope of outpacing the allosaurid, and its best defence lies in hunkering down so that the upper armour protects its only weak spot – a soft underbelly. The allosaurid paces around the spiny mound, sniffing intently through broad nostrils. Shoving hard with its snout it attempts to roll the ankylosaur – no such luck. Then, baring 60 long, pointed teeth, it takes a fierce bite across the small of the ankylosaur's back. But the teeth cannot penetrate the armour, and so the allosaurid strides away, defeated and still hungry, leaving the ankylosaur to survive another day.

Though it sounds like a scene from *Jurassic Park*, it is not so fanciful; there are fossils to prove that dinosaurs such as these once lived and died on the land mass we know today as New Zealand. But how did the dinosaurs get here?

From Pangaea to Zealandia

Movement of heat deep within the Earth causes the plates that cover its surface to creep in all directions; they drift apart, collide, grind past one another, ride over or under each other, slowly but with immeasurable power. Over the billions of years of Earth's history land masses have joined into supercontinents and rifted apart again in a continuous process of change. Some 251 million years ago, at the dawn of the Mesozoic era, all of the continents were joined together in a single huge mass called Pangaea ('all land'), which lay amid Panthalassa ('all ocean'). The weather was relatively dry and warm, and huge deserts covered much of the planet's surface. Occasional monsoons provided much-

Opposite: Some New Zealand dinosaurs of the Cretaceous. A slow-moving, plant-eating ankylosaur (left) squats to protect its soft underbelly, exposing only its bony armour plating to the meat-eating allosaurid (right) that approaches. Hypsilophodont dinosaurs (background) would have used speed to escape predators; their bodies were supported on sturdy legs counterbalanced by a long, stiff tail.

needed rain, and so the ancestors of today's plants and animals were able to thrive and evolve. Twenty million years later, dinosaurs first appeared on Earth; and all through their reign of over 160 million years, the land masses would continue to undergo change.

By the end of the Triassic period (251–200 million years ago), Pangaea had divided into two: Laurasia lay in the northern hemisphere, while to the south Gondwana comprised the vast land masses that would later become South America, India, South Africa, Antarctica, New Guinea, Australia and New Zealand. The wet, warm climate enabled the evolution of huge trees as well as ferns and low-growing plants.

New Zealand as we now know it was a tiny portion of a very much larger continental land mass attached to eastern Gondwana. Geologists refer to this land mass as Zealandia. At the beginning of the Cretaceous period (146–65 million years ago), Zealandia was truly enormous. It stretched west to what is now the Lord Howe Rise, north to New Caledonia, east to the Chatham Islands, and south to the Campbell Plateau: in all, an area of about half the size of modern-day Australia. Then, as now, Zealandia lay directly over the boundary between the Australian and Pacific plates.

Neither the Southern Ocean nor the Tasman Sea existed in the early Cretaceous; Zealandia was attached to Australia and Antarctica, and Antarctica connected to South America. This enabled the spreading of plants that had evolved on Gondwana in the warm Triassic period, including those, such as horsetails, ferns, lycopods and clubmosses, that would feature among the later plants of New Zealand. Present, too, were the ancestors of today's podocarps – trees such as totara, kahikatea and rimu – and the kauri.

Dinosaurs

At that time, too, millions of dinosaurs roamed over the entire Gondwanan (and Laurasian) land masses. Tectonic movement caused Gondwana to break up, the land masses drifting apart. Panthalassa flooded into the widening valleys, creating the beginnings of many of today's great oceans. And then it happened: 83 million years ago the land mass of Zealandia finally broke away from what was left of Gondwana, and rather like an extraordinary Noah's Ark it drifted off into the South Pacific. The long isolation had begun. On board Zealandia were all the plants, dinosaurs and other animals that had existed in the south-east corner of Gondwana.

Not until 1980 were the first dinosaur fossils found in

Below: A map of how the eastern parts of the ancient southern supercontinent Gondwana may have looked some 80 million years ago. Zealandia extends north to New Caledonia and south to the subantarctic islands, covering a total area of more than 3.5 million square kilometres. It is shown here having just separated from the Australia–Antarctica portion of Gondwana. The pale tints represent continental margins over which animals and plants would have been able to disperse. (After Gibbs 2007)

New Zealand, and even now very little evidence of dinosaurs has turned up in our rocks. Fossil remains do, however, tell us that much of mid-Cretaceous Zealandia was covered with a primeval forest that mainly contained ferns, cycads and conifers, although the seeds of new flowering plants – angiosperms – were no doubt arriving on the winds. Ancestors of the tuatara were already present, as were several species of primitive frog, the ancient giant snails and the ancestors of today's weta. It is believed that several endemic bird species also arrived at this time.

While rifting from Gondwana, Zealandia stretched and thinned and cooled down, and in so doing it lost buoyancy and began to sink slowly into the ocean. The series of islands we now call New Zealand is made up of the peaks of this land mass; altogether, the emergent points occupy just 7 per cent of the original area that existed at the beginning of the Cretaceous. Around these shores now lies the largest drowned continent that ever existed on Earth; an 'Atlantis' of enormous proportions, on whose terrain dinosaurs once roamed. Listed below are some of the dinosaurs whose fossils have so far been discovered here.

Ankylosaurs

Ankylosaurs were plant-eating dinosaurs that stood on all fours, with upperparts covered from head to tail by sheets of thick bony armour. Ankylosaurs evolved during the late Jurassic period, and by the Cretaceous period there were species with especially tough armour; some had a heavy club at the tip of the tail. They were widespread in the northern hemisphere, but, so far, just two ankylosaur fossils have been found in New Zealand; they are from a species that lacked the tail club, possibly the same species whose fossils have been found in Australia.

Hypsilophodontids

Barely 1 metre tall and around 3 metres long, hypsilophodontids ran on their hind legs, their body balanced by the long, stiff tail, and would have used agility and speed to escape large predators. They may have lived in herds, and fed on low-growing plants, processing the fodder with strong cheek muscles and chewing teeth. Hypsilophodont fossils have been found on almost every continent.

Allosaurids

Allosaurids were giant theropods – dinosaurs that walked on their hind limbs – and numbered among the largest land carnivores that ever lived, measuring 8 metres long and weighing well over 1 tonne. They had huge heads, and muscular hind limbs, but their arms were short, with only three fingers per hand, each digit tipped with an 8-centimetre claw. Allosaurids are thought to have hunted in packs, and despite their size they could probably have managed bursts of speeds up to 30 kilometres per hour. Fossils have been found in North America, Portugal, Australia and New Zealand.

FLOWERS AND INSECTS

By the middle Cretaceous, groups of insects such as butterflies, grasshoppers, aphids, ants, wasps and bees, which had first appeared in the early Cretaceous period, grew in number. Some flew across the slowly widening Tasman Sea assisted by a strong prevailing westerly wind, a journey that airborne creatures make to this day. The global rise of the insects coincided with the rise of flowering plants, forging an association in which certain insects (such as bees) came to rely on flowers for food, while flowers came to rely on insects (as well as birds, and the wind) for pollination.

Chapter 2

BENEATH CRETACEOUS SEAS

83–65 million years ago

THE SEAS THAT WASHED ZEALANDIA'S SHORES during the mid- to late Cretaceous held a wide range of marine life forms; we would recognise many of them, since their descendants – crustaceans, bivalves, sponges, sharks and bony fishes, to name just a few – survive today. But there also lived a number of vastly different creatures, few of which were more spectacular than the marine reptiles. These creatures are all the more interesting for the fact that they were descended from common ancestors that lived in the sea around 400 million years ago during the Carboniferous period, but later developed into vertebrate life forms that began to live – successfully – on land, before eventually returning to the water.

The first vertebrates to crawl out of the Carboniferous seas were the world's earliest amphibians. One such was *Acanthostega*, a creature that looked like a fish with four legs. The amphibians continued to catch their food in the sea or in lakes, using their gills to 'breathe' in the water. Like the fish from which they evolved, they laid eggs in ponds and streams. When their eggs hatched, the young went through the tadpole stage, breathing under water through feathery gills. But as these amphibians grew to adult size, they developed lungs that enabled them to spend more time on land. However, they also faced a problem in that every time they entered the water to feed on small fish, be it pond, stream or ocean, these places were also teeming with larger fish whose diet included eggs, tadpoles … even adult amphibians. To some degree, dry land was a friendlier environment than water for these proto-amphibians. The more time they spent on *terra firma*, the safer they were.

And so the amphibians began to evolve the vital characteristics that would be passed on to the land-dwelling reptiles. These included a tough moisture-retaining skin; an egg protected by an amnion (water-retaining membrane) and a leathery shell; and the ability to expand and contract the rib-cage – in short, to breathe. (Fossils found in Nova Scotia, some 200 million years old, come from slim lizard-like creatures that represent this 'stepping-stone' stage between amphibians and reptiles. They lacked webbed toes, and had cylindrical tails that were obviously pointed.) Quadrupeds were rapidly evolving into ever larger forms, and were also colonising deserts where amphibians could not survive.

These reptiles were still 'cold-blooded', however, and became cold and immobile at night, basking in the sunlight after daybreak to warm their bodies

Opposite: Among Cretaceous marine reptiles, some had evolved large bodies with streamlined profiles. Clockwise from top right: Elasmosaurus, pliosaur, ichthyosaur, giant turtle (Archelon), Mixosaurus, mosasaur.

into activity. To avoid overheating, they rested in the shade of plants and tree ferns. They had become hunters and plant-eaters; the age of the giant reptiles had dawned. A branch of reptiles would evolve to become dinosaurs, while others, which still had an aquatic lifestyle, daily returned to the water to hunt fish, spending more and more time in the sea. And so, gradually, these land reptiles went full circle and evolved into marine reptiles (see panel, left). Probably the first to return to the sea were the ancestors of today's turtles; to combat the resistance they encountered when they began moving through the water, their shells evolved quickly to become flatter and more streamlined. At least 20 animal groups reverted to an aquatic lifestyle during the age of the dinosaurs – crocodiles and turtles are probably their only descendants living today.

Below are some examples of the more noteworthy groups of marine reptiles and other life forms known from the Cretaceous seas of Zealandia.

Plesiosaurs and elasmosaurs

Marine reptiles evolved smooth body forms allowing fast, friction-free passage through water, and many became a great deal larger than their land-based ancestors. After all, immersion in water liberates the body and its organs from the constricting effects of gravity. The plesiosaurs, a group dating from the early Jurassic period, are a case in point. They had a long neck and short tail, and propelled themselves by means of four paddle-like limbs. By the Cretaceous they included *Elasmosaurus*, whose neck accounted for two-thirds of the animal's overall length of 9 metres. Whereas we humans have seven neck vertebrae, *Elasmosaurus* had 75! The snake-like neck ended in a very small head, which was possibly held above the water surface in order to reduce water resistance and to enable the reptile to spot nearby fish and other marine creatures from above, which it would then hunt down and trap with its long, very sharp teeth. Gastroliths (stomach stones) have been found along with bone fossils, giving weight to the theory that *Elasmosaurus* swallowed these stones. They would have helped break down the food it swallowed. (Moa also swallowed stones, to similar effect.) The finest New Zealand example to date of an elasmosaur was discovered at Shag Point, North Otago, in 1983 by Ewan Fordyce, and is now housed in the Otago Museum in Dunedin.

Pliosaurs

Pliosaurs were top Cretaceous predators. One species, *Kronosaurus*, was first discovered in Australia during the 1880s; Queensland cattle ranchers came across its fossil bones protruding from the ground like great bleached tree roots. The overall body length was a little more than 14 metres, and the skull alone topped 3.5 metres. Viciously toothed jaws would have enabled *Kronosaurus* to overcome animals its own size in the manner of today's great white sharks. It is also possible that a pliosaur swam with its mouth open so that water was then directed up to the roof of its mouth, where it would pass over smell sensors and out through the nostrils. This would have enabled the pliosaur to detect odours in the water in the same way that modern sharks 'smell' the water. Although a large pliosaur fossil was found in New Zealand in 1859, and fragments of pliosaurian fossils have since been discovered in North Canterbury and Hawke's Bay, they probably belonged to a smaller reptile than the great *Kronosaurus*, one that lived in Gondwanan waters until about 98 million years ago.

Ichthyosaurs and *Mixosaurus*

Ichthyosaur, meaning 'fish lizard', was another name given to a type of marine reptile recently discovered as a fossil. However, the name is a misnomer, as this creature was an air-breathing, marine reptile – not a fish. It had a body shape that was not unlike that of today's dolphins, and like today's dolphins and whales, an ichthyosaur gave birth in the sea. Barely 1 metre long, it propelled itself by thrusts of its vertically lobed tail, and had a long snout equipped with many sharp teeth, so it must have been a fast-swimming predator, possibly reaching speeds near 40 kilometres per hour and able to catch the many fish species that swam in Cretaceous seas. What were thought to be the first New Zealand ichthyosaur fossils were collected in 1873 from Triassic rocks in North Island's Marokopa District, and were posted to England for identification. Sadly, no further examination of the fossils took place because the sailing ship *Matoaka* transporting this precious cargo was lost at sea.

Above: A Cretaceous ichthyosaur, about 1 metre long. Some of the earlier ichthyosaurs of the Triassic were much larger, reaching lengths of up to 15 metres.

By the Cretaceous period the ichthyosaurs were nearing the end of their time on Earth, which had peaked much earlier in the late Triassic and early Jurassic periods. One early form of ichthyosaur, from the middle Triassic, was *Mixosaurus* ('mixed lizard'). Fossils have turned up worldwide, from Europe to China and North America as well as New Zealand, so it was obviously a very successful animal. This marine reptile was probably a fast swimmer that lived on a diet of fish, its speed aided by limbs that were used not as paddles but as steering devices. Unlike other ichthyosaurs, *Mixosaurus* had a long, slender and pointed tail.

Mosasaurs

Some of the most interesting marine fossils found in New Zealand had the shortest time on Earth. Mosasaurs evolved in the late Cretaceous, but disappeared 65 million years ago along with the dinosaurs and many marine reptiles. These were probably the largest marine reptiles that lived at that time, and were true lizards – marine lizards. Their skin was scaly and they cruised through the water by undulating their body in the manner of today's crocodiles. With such a body shape, they could not have progressed far on land, so probably gave birth to live young in the ocean. Some mosasaurs grew up to 9 metres long, and would have shared many characteristics with the world's largest living land reptile, the Komodo dragon, which is a top predator on its island homes in Indonesia. Mosasaur fossils were first found in New Zealand in 1869, but the group is known worldwide. To date, six genera and eight species have been described, of which three genera are known only from New Zealand.

Above: Belemnites swam in the world's oceans for 200 million years and became extinct at the end of the Cretaceous period, 65 million years ago. They are thought to be the ancestors of today's squid and cuttlefish – which, outwardly at least, they closely resemble.
Below: A New Zealand arrow squid (Nototodarus sloanii).

Turtles

The turtles are part of a group known as chelonians, which also includes the tortoises. Chelonians first appeared about 215 million years ago during the Triassic period, around the time the dinosaurs made their debut; but these marine reptiles have of course enjoyed by far the longer reign: today there are more than 300 living chelonian species. As Professor Michael Benton of the University of Bristol puts it, 'It seems that early on they hit upon a successful design, the "shell", and stayed with it.' The largest ancestral chelonian, known as *Archelon*, weighed about 3 tonnes and was at least 4.5 metres long. Its jaws were toothless and instead sported a beak, which was more than sharp enough for its normal diet of soft-bodied animals, such as jellyfish, and could even crush ammonites (see panel, opposite). This super-turtle roamed the world's seas, including, no doubt, those fringing Gondwana, during the late Cretaceous period. Like all marine turtles, only the female came ashore – to lay her eggs.

The fossils of *Archelon* have been found mainly in North America in dry-land areas that were once flooded by shallow seas. Today's two species of Ridley sea turtle (genus *Lepidochelys*), which live at tropical latitudes in the Atlantic and Pacific oceans, are linked with *Lepidochelys waikatoica*, a turtle ancestor found as a fossil in the Port Waikato rocks of the North Island.

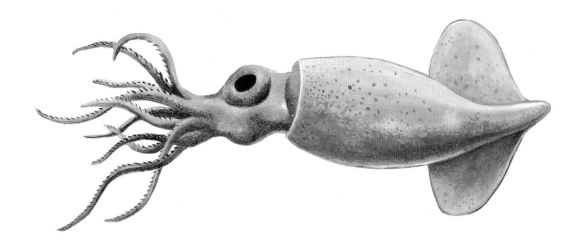

AMMONITES: PLINY'S 'HORN OF AMMON'

Outnumbering marine reptiles and fish by a huge order of magnitude were the invertebrates of Zealandian seas. Among others these included sponges, echinoderms (such as sea urchins and sea stars), molluscs, crustaceans and cephalopods. This last order of animals today includes octopus, squid and cuttlefish, and among their extinct relatives were the remarkable ammonites. Pliny the Elder, who died in AD 79, studied fossil ammonites from the Mediterranean and named them *Ammonis cornus*, or 'horn of Ammon', after the Egyptian god Ammon, who is usually pictured as a man with ram's horns.

Ammonites were around for a very long time indeed, evolving around the early Devonian period, some 400 million years ago. For many years their fossils have been turning up in various countries around the world, including New Zealand, where like many organisms they finally became extinct during the great die-off that occurred 65 million years ago (see Chapter 4). Ammonite fossils look much like the nautilus, a modern-day cephalopod that has remained unchanged for millions of years and is named after the Greek word meaning 'sailor'. (A cephalopod is a marine mollusc with a head surrounded by tentacles.) The ammonite's closest living relative is not, however, the nautilus, but the octopus, squid and cuttlefish. Coiled ammonites appear to have evolved from an uncoiled form, and many were thought to have been strong swimmers with good eyesight, and with streamlined shells that were discus-shaped. (An ammonite fossil was probably the original discus used by Ancient Greeks in their Olympic Games.) Interestingly, ammonite fossils have been found with bite marks on their shells which match the teeth of mosasaurs.

When an ammonite died, it sank to the sea floor and was buried in sediment; but if it was buried in clay, its original shell coating of mother-of-pearl was often well preserved. Fossils turn up reasonably often in New Zealand's rocks, and in 1978 the NZ Geological Survey discovered the largest specimen ever found here, preserved in Jurassic rocks some 142 million years old; the fossil is almost 1.5 metres across. West Germany lays claim to the largest recorded ammonite fossil, with a shell of 2.55 metres in diameter. A recent claim for a larger specimen in British Columbia has yet to be authenticated.

Left: Fossils of the ammonite illustrated, which swam in Jurassic and Cretaceous seas around the world, often turn up in New Zealand. They tend to average 50–200 millimetres in diameter. Rather like a modern submarine, an ammonite shifted gas in and out of its shell chambers to help it rise, sink or remain suspended with neutral buoyancy in the water.

Chapter 3

CRETACEOUS COASTS

83–65 million years ago

Above: Cycads would have been a food source for dinosaurs. Fossilised remains of ancient cycad forms closely resemble their modern-day descendants. Opposite: In this scene showing a sauropod family under attack from a megalosaur, an estuary is flanked with small stands of mangroves; ancestors of today's mangroves, these trees grew well in the muddy sand and brackish water, and like today's mangroves they were partially submerged twice a day. Further up the shore grows a thicket of horsetails. In the distance a rocky outcrop provides nesting sites for a breeding colony of long-tailed, fish-eating pterosaurs. A lone pterosaur glides overhead, while another skim-feeds near the shore.

WELL INTO THE LATE CRETACEOUS PERIOD, Zealandia's coastal forests were home to cycads – ancient plants that have been around for nearly 300 million years. In the early Triassic, when dinosaurs first appeared, cycads made up 20 per cent of the world's flora. Their fossils have been found in Alaska, Africa, Australia, Argentina, the British Isles, Antarctica and New Zealand.

By the time Zealandia rifted away from Gondwana 83 million years ago, however, cycads were beginning to rub shoulders with the conifers we know today as podocarps: trees whose descendants we know as totara, rimu, kahikatea, miro and matai. There was also the ancestor of the largest of the southern hemisphere conifers, the mighty kauri (*Agathis australis*); whose modern relatives in the same family include the Queensland kauri pine, the Norfolk Island pine, the South American monkey puzzle tree and the Australian bunya pines.

In addition to 11 living genera of cycads worldwide, 19 extinct genera have been described. Cycads are gymnosperms – plants whose ovules are borne naked on the scales of their cones. One of their most interesting features is the enormous amount of pollen produced by the male trees, providing a fascinating early example of wind pollination. The pollen was produced inside large cone-like arrangements that sat in the centre of a cycad's rosette of palm-like fronds. A stiff breeze was all that was needed for the pollen to be distributed to nearby plants. This ancient method of wind pollination is still used today by conifers.

Cycads would have been a favourite food of dinosaurs; plant-eating dinosaur species outnumbered the meat-eaters by about 30 to one. Pollen is also nutritious and would have appealed to small dinosaurs as a food source.

Some species of cycad had one more method by which they ensured their pollen would be distributed. Insects were diversifying rapidly during the Cretaceous, and the warmth of a cycad's cones would have attracted weevils and bees that feasted on the powder and became liberally covered with it at the same time. The insects would then move to another cycad cone to continue feeding, transferring pollen and thereby fertilising the second cycad far more successfully than if it had depended upon chance dispersal by wind.

Great changes occurred in Zealandia's flora during the Cretaceous when cycads, ginkgos and some conifers either declined in numbers or became locally extinct, possibly due to competition with flowering plants, which were then

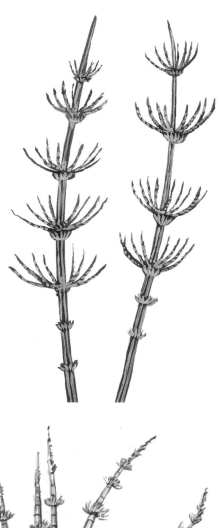

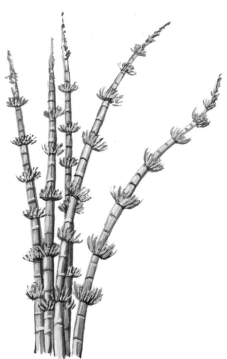

Above: Horsetails. These primitive and rugged plants, which have changed little in 300 million years, would have been a likely food source for dinosaurs.

on the rise. The landscape was largely low-lying and gently contoured, and the warm, humid climate was perfect for nurturing dense, wet forest. In time the low-lying coastal terrain became swamp. Vast quantities of fallen plant material was buried in acidic conditions, creating the ideal environment for the development of peat. Over long periods of time, buried peat becomes lignite coal (which is mined so productively in places like Greymouth today).

Plants that were relatively abundant in Cretaceous Zealandia included the ancestors of today's tree ferns (similar to modern *Cyathea* and *Dicksonia* species), ground ferns and lycopodiums or clubmosses. Lycopodiums are modest in size today, but during the Carboniferous period they grew to the size of large forest trees.

The primitive horsetail

One plant that also no doubt provided sauropod dinosaurs with a food supply was the horsetail. This vascular plant, whose descendants survive today in the genus *Equisetum*, produces whorls of slender jointed stems. Horsetail has an ancient lineage, and its method of breeding is as primitive as its appearance. It thrived during the Carboniferous period 300 million years ago, and its buried remains today have provided humankind with extensive coal deposits.

The stems of horsetails grew quickly from underground rhizomes (root-like stems), which would not have been disturbed by grazing dinosaurs. This meant that after much of the exposed plant was eaten by a sauropod, a horsetail could quickly regenerate. Today, the descendants of horsetails grow in all tropical and temperate regions including New Zealand and Australia. While some of the now-extinct species probably grew in large thickets with trees reaching more than 20 metres tall, the tallest species alive today grows in South America and barely reaches 10 metres. Several North American species are known as the scouring rush; they have a high silica content, which is extracted and used in scouring liquids and abrasive powders.

One of the common horsetail descendants found today in New Zealand and Australia is *Leptocarpus similis,* commonly known as jointed wire rush; and like the original horsetail plant it is also leafless. Another horsetail that is native to the northern hemisphere but has become established and widespread in watercourses throughout New Zealand is the field horsetail (*Equisetum arvense*). Ironically, it is toxic to horses, as well as being an environmental pest.

Rise of the flowering plants

The Cretaceous also witnessed the rise of angiosperms (flowering plants), which evolved on Gondwana shortly before Zealandia rifted away. Their ability to reproduce rapidly ensured that they spread and diversified swiftly. One of the very first flowering plants to appear in Zealandia was *Ascaerina lucida*, known today by its Maori name hutu. This small aromatic tree has thin red branches and beautiful yellow-green foliage. The tooth-margined leaves are carried on long petioles or stems, and from a distance appear to be quite feathery. Also growing in these ancient coastal forests were the ancestors of such plants as the southern beech, grass trees, pepper trees, buttercups and celery pines.

The beautiful magnolia we know today is one of the earliest of all flowering plants, and has probably changed little since it appeared during the Cretaceous. Unlike other prehistoric plants, magnolia leaves were very juicy and nutritious. No doubt when it flowered, dinosaurs were attracted by its beautiful perfume and so browsed the fleshy petals as well as the leaves.

Other plants of Gondwanan origin whose descendants still splash our forests with their colourful presence include members of the protea family, Proteaceae. These include the small tree known as toru, which in October swathes its branches with clumps of small yellow-and-gold flowers; and the 30-metre-tall rewarewa tree, whose blooms are like no other flowering plant – 30 to 50 flowers coiled in every direction and densely packed into a 100-millimetre-long cluster with protruding stamens, the whole flower looking like a floral porcupine.

These plants were the ancestors of modern plants, and although they looked similar, they were not quite the same. Another plant, whose ancestors grew thickly along the coastal margins of Zealandia, was itself an ancestor of today's mangroves. These salt-tolerant 'rainforests of the sea' are believed to have originated in the Indo-Malayan region, since there are more species there than anywhere else on Earth. The secret of their success at spreading around the world is the simple fact that mangrove seed capsules float. It is likely that they floated to Zealandia at about the time that it parted from Gondwana.

Fingertip flight

Flying over the thickets of mangroves on their way to the open sea, where they skimmed over the waves to scoop up fish, were flying reptiles known as pterosaurs. These were not dinosaurs, and they glided and flew on wings of skin stretched from one long finger of each forelimb.

Pterosaurs came in different sizes. The largest species, known to science as *Quetzalcoatlus*, had a wingspan of 12 metres – greater than that of a hang-glider. Appropriately enough, its fossils have only been found in Texas! By contrast, the pterosaur fossils known from two fragments found in New Zealand had a spread of about 4 metres. Smaller still was the fossil of a pterosaur discovered in Asia in the 1960s. A skeleton of the type named *Sordes* was later discovered in lake

Above: Magnolias were among the first of the world's flowering plants, judging from fossils that date back some 95 million years. As with horsetails, their leaves would have been eaten by dinosaurs. Below: It is generally believed that mangroves have been growing on the New Zealand land mass since it parted from Gondwana some 80 million years ago. A sprouting seed lies at the base of the young plant.

deposits in Kazakhstan during the 1970s. This small pterosaur was covered with fine fur that was 6 millimetres long, and had a long jaw lined with many small, sharp teeth; hence it was probably an insect hunter. Some palaeontologists have taken this as evidence that ancient pterosaurs were warm-blooded. Their wings were formed from very tough skin, and their bones, like those of most modern birds, were hollow and honeycombed inside so as to save weight.

Sauropods – a long vegetarian lunch

The flatter coastal lands were no doubt the favoured haunts of our largest plant-eating dinosaur, a 12-metre sauropod similar to *Diplodocus*. Sauropods include the world's largest dinosaurs. A recent North American find may be as much as 40 metres long, and two titanosaurid sauropods found in Queensland in 2005–6 are around 25 metres in length.

The typical sauropod had a small head, long neck, large elephantine body and legs like tree trunks; it also had an extremely long whip-like tail which was no doubt used defensively when under attack from flesh-eating theropod dinosaurs. The dinosaur could move its neck not only up and down but also from side to side, and probably held it in a horizontal position except when raising it high to browse treetop foliage or fruit, which it 'raked' in by means of the long, rod-like teeth in the front of its jaws.

Theropods

Theropods fit the basic bipedal body plan exemplified by such dinosaurs as *Velociraptor* and *Tyrannosaurus rex*. They ran on their hind limbs, had small arms and a massive skull, balanced by a tail held stiffly out behind. Some species carried horns and crests on their head. Most, though not all, were meat-eaters.

Theropods have an interesting history of discovery. The theropod *Megalosaurus*, or 'great lizard', was the first dinosaur to be named. The lower part of a fossil thighbone of this animal was discovered in England in 1676. Its identity remained a mystery until the 1820s, when French anatomist Georges Cuvier correctly attributed the bone to a huge lizard-like animal, which was later christened by William Buckland, Professor of Geology at the University of Oxford. Later, *Megalosaurus* was among a select number of species cited by Richard Owen, a brilliant British anatomist and palaeontologist, who announced his discovery of a new category of extinct reptiles, which in 1842 he christened the Dinosauria, or 'terrible lizards'.

Megalosaurs were one of the first dinosaurs to be found in New Zealand, one of a number of discoveries made by the dinosaur hunter Joan Wiffen during the mid-1970s. A fossil tail vertebra from Hawke's Bay indicated a theropod approximately half a tonne in weight and about 4 metres in length. With its tail held high, it probably moved rapidly on its large hind legs in order to 'run down' its prey, although it is unlikely to have maintained a high speed for long.

Opposite: Fossil records show that ancestors of the kauri tree were already in existence more than 200 million years ago. These same records show that although it has evolved into several Asian and South Pacific species, the kauri has changed little over time. The New Zealand kauri species is the most ancient of all; it is also the largest.

Chapter 4

WHEN THE WORLD NEARLY ENDED

65 million years ago

BY THE LATE CRETACEOUS PERIOD there were more than 1,000 different dinosaur species on the various land masses – including Zealandia – that had once been part of Gondwana. These reptiles had ruled the Earth for 175 million years, but 65 million years ago their reign was abruptly terminated. In a very short space of time, geologically speaking, some 70 per cent of the planet's species died out. This mass extinction marked the end of the Mesozoic era and the dawn of the Cenozoic era, the age of mammals.

What killed the dinosaurs?

The cause of the mass extinction may have been a huge asteroid, some 10 kilometres across, which crashed into the Gulf of Mexico and the Yucatan Peninsula. It may not sound huge, but its velocity – about 10 kilometres per second – was such that the asteroid left an impact crater about 200 kilometres across.

What were the effects of such a large asteroid slamming into Earth at over 50,000 kilometres an hour? The pressure wave created by the asteroid tearing through Earth's atmosphere produced such intense heat that widespread forest fires broke out. On impact, an estimated 321,840 cubic kilometres of Earth's surface was immediately vaporised. Earth's climate was profoundly altered. Clouds of choking dust encircled the planet, and a darkness lasting for six months would have descended over the land and oceans. The asteroid landed in an area that was rich in sulphur, and so when this was blown into the atmosphere it would have combined with moisture and returned to Earth as sulphuric acid; the entire globe would have had heavy falls of acid rain.

Bereft of sunlight, plants died. In the seas, too, photosynthesising plankton were likewise snuffed out. As a result, a huge food source was lost to terrestrial plant-eaters, and likewise to marine plankton feeders, severely disrupting food chains on land and sea. Although marine creatures would have initially been protected from the firestorms, they would not have survived the lack of food once the plankton and the plankton-eaters died out. Also, many would have been adversely affected by the large amounts of acid rain that fell into the sea.

Today, the Mexican impact crater lies some 12,000 kilometres from New Zealand; in Cretaceous times, however, Zealandia's geographical location was probably closer. The asteroid's impact also generated a colossal tsunami up to

Opposite: Many scientists believe that the violent impact of a massive asteroid on the coast of what is now Yucatan, Mexico, 66 million years ago heralded the beginning of the end for the dinosaurs. The cataclysm would have caused widespread forest fires and tsunamis, and the clouds of dust and smoke would have created a 'nuclear winter' lasting several months, starving plants of essential sunlight.

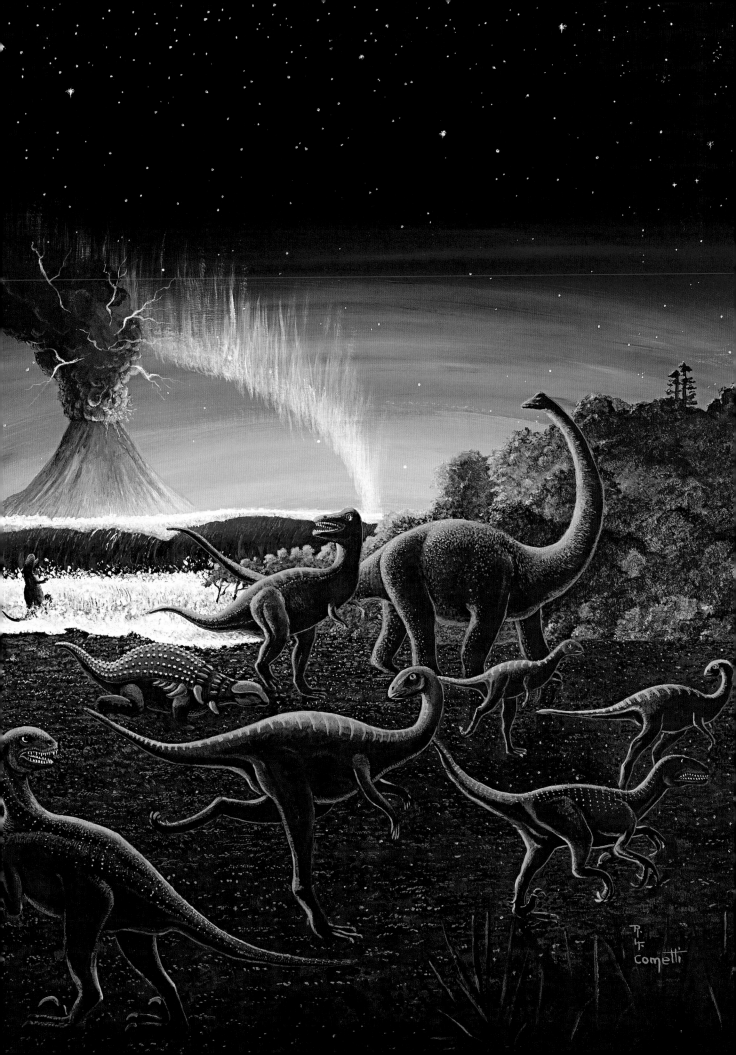

2 kilometres high, a 'Mexican wave' that raced across the Atlantic and Pacific oceans; the first sizeable land mass that it swamped would have been Zealandia. While there is no hard evidence of the effects of this tsunami, there is plenty of evidence of the atmospheric fallout from the impact.

Elementary evidence

Asteroids contain far greater quantities of the elements iridium and palladium than are found naturally on Earth, and 65 million years ago a soil layer was laid down all around the globe which contains abnormally high quantities of these two elements. (This layer was noted in 1980 by US geologist Walter Alvarez and his father, Luis, who had been studying a sample in Italy. It was the Alvarez team, in fact, who first proposed the theory of an asteroid coming to Earth and causing mass extinction – a theory that was widely accepted in 1990 after the discovery of the Mexican impact crater.) Scientists led by Chris Hollis, a paleontologist with GNS Science, recently studied the rock layer in several New Zealand locations. Hollis announced that 'New Zealand has the only southern hemisphere record of the extinction event across a wide range of environments.' This rock layer can tell us a lot about what happened 65 million years ago. It contains large amounts of soot, which indicates widespread outbreaks of forest fires. It also has a lot of fern spores, but very little pollen from mixed forest vegetation, revealing that while flowering plants and conifers were decimated, ferns fairly rapidly took their place. (Rapid, at least, in geological terms: the fern takeover took some tens of thousands of years!)

The mass extinction of 65 million years ago, dividing the Cretaceous period from the Cenozoic era, is known as the K–T Boundary; the name comes from the Latin word *creta* (chalk) and Tertiary, the former name for the Cenozoic. When the asteroid hit Earth, huge quantities of a chalky dust rained down all over Earth as a result of the fallout, hence the name Cretaceous. To date, there have been at least five mass extinctions during Earth's 4.6-billion-year existence. The most severe was the Permian–Triassic, 251 million years ago, which scientists often call 'The Great Dying' because so much of life on Earth was wiped out – and all within the space of less than 100,000 years. What caused it? It happened so long ago that hard evidence is scarce. Scientists do, however, have a few theories. At the time, all the land masses were joined in one supercontinent, an arrangement that would have obstructed ocean currents, leading to a degree of stagnation in the oceans. Also, many volcanoes were erupting, creating a 'greenhouse effect' much like the one described earlier. And, finally, scientists have found chemical traces in Permian–Triassic rocks that again point the finger at an asteroid strike. Perhaps all of these factors – stagnation, global warming, sudden impact – combined to make life on Earth near impossible.

What is in no doubt is the close link between episodes of volcanism and periods of climate change. In 2007 a report in the journal *Science* gave evidence of another cataclysmic event that occurred 55 million years ago after a further series of enormous volcanic eruptions were responsible for sending more than 2,000 gigatonnes of carbon dioxide and methane into the atmosphere. This resulted in rapid global warming on an unprecedented scale. The event is referred to as PETM, or the Paleocene–Eocene Thermal Maximum, and the effects of the eruptions influenced Earth's temperatures for approximately 220,000 years. Temperatures in the Arctic increased by 8–10°C, and the rest of the world experienced a temperature rise of at least 5°C. This event also caused the acid content of the world's oceans to rise dramatically, which possibly dissolved the shells of many marine creatures, contributing to their extinction. (Global warming events such as these, which have punctuated Earth's long history, cannot be compared to the dramatic increase in temperatures that we are currently experiencing, as today's global warming has been caused entirely by humankind.)

Despite the worldwide catastrophe of 65 million years ago, not all of Earth's animals and plants died out. It would have taken many years for the dust storms to subside, allowing the sun to shine once more. Some dinosaur species appear to have lived on for a number of years. Frogs, crocodiles and alligators pulled through, despite widespread losses, as did insects and of course a number of plants, including many flowering species. Mammals, too, survived, and over the next few million years would evolve to fill the niches left by the vanished dinosaurs – except in Zealandia where there were almost no mammals, and birds evolved in a way that was not only unprecedented but also unique.

What would our post-apocalyptic Zealandia have looked like? It had become a rather barren archipelago, much like the rest of the world. There is little evidence of local volcanic activity. The dinosaurs had gone; there were no longer herds of fleet-footed hypsilophodontids flitting through our forests, nor graceful sauropods browsing on forest plants; and all the other species of land dinosaurs, plus the flying reptiles, would have disappeared. Recently, fossil fragments of a huge crocodile, one of a group known as the mekosuchines (see Chapter 7),

… OR WAS IT THE DECCAN TRAPS?

There is a strong possibility that the Mexico asteroid alone was not to blame for the dinosaurs' passing. A couple of million years or so before the asteroid struck, there was an extraordinarily high level of volcanic activity in an area known as the Deccan Traps, which are located on the west-central plateau of India and are one of the largest volcanic features on Earth. This produced a vast outpouring of basaltic lava, which today measures more than half a million cubic kilometres in total. The basalt flooding pumped gigatonnes of gases (mostly carbon dioxide and suphur dioxide) into the atmosphere, causing global sea and air temperatures to rise by several degrees Celsius, poisoning and choking life forms. Many scientists credit the Deccan volcanism with the extinction of the dinosaurs, or at least playing a major hand in it.

were found in Central Otago's Miocene deposits, which suggests that at least some reptiles were present then. The only mammal that reached New Zealand at that time was the ancestor of the short-tailed bat; the long-tailed bat would not arrive until millions of years later. That said, in 2006 fossil fragments of a mouse-sized land mammal of unknown affinity were discovered in a Miocene site at St Bathans, Central Otago, which refutes the long-held belief that New Zealand has, but for its little bats, been entirely free of terrestrial mammals.

The dinosaurs that lived

Meanwhile, birds were – excuse the pun – waiting in the wings. For it is now believed that dinosaurs did not completely die out 65 million years ago. One branch of smallish reptiles living in the world's colder climates had long since began to produce feathers in order to keep warm. Firstly, these feathers were short and fluffy and had good insulating properties. Millions of years later, these insulating feathers evolved to become flight feathers used for gliding, and eventually for flight. Feathers are made from keratin, the fibrous protein from which nails, hair and scales are produced, and this protein is present in all animals.

More than 100 million years before the K–T Boundary, a creature named *Archaeopteryx* had evolved in the late Jurassic period. Its beak had teeth, and its tail was long and bony, and its famous fossil (discovered in 1861) showed the unmistakable outline of feathers. And feathers apart, the fossil skeleton of *Archaeopteryx* showed it to be almost identical to the fossil of *Compsognathus*, a theropod dinosaur. In 1996 another feathered dinosaur fossil was discovered in Liaoning, China, which had lived more recently than *Archaeopteryx*. This new fossil was given the name *Sinosauropteryx*. It had a downy plumage and a feathery crest running from its neck down to the small of its back. The 'feathers' were single strands – thousands of them – and as such were more like fur than feathers, but were clearly a giant leap forward from the usual reptile scales. This feathered dinosaur probably chased its prey and leapt into the air to catch them.

Insects were surely on the menu, but one fossil find comes complete with its last meal – a small mammal.

Sinosauropteryx possessed grasping forelimbs, which evidently fell short of serving as wings capable of flight. An interesting fossil found in 1998, also at Liaoning, may hold a clue to how forelimbs evolved into wings. *Caudipteryx* was about 1 metre long, the same size as *Sinosauropteryx*, but clearly visible on its forelimbs and tail were long, trailing feathers. It is not clear what the proto-wings were used for; maybe they helped *Caudipteryx* stay balanced while running. Over millions of years, these feathers would have become longer until, eventually, feathered dinosaurs were capable of gliding. Evolution rarely takes a holiday unless there is no longer room for improvement. And some families of these fully feathered, flying dinosaurs survived to this day – we call them birds!

*Left: The kokako (*Callaeas cinerea*) was once widespread in the forests of both islands, but in two forms. The North Island species had blue wattles; the South Island bird, which also lived on Stewart Island/Rakiura and is now believed to be extinct, had orange wattles. Although kokako are still endangered, they have now been relocated to mainland sanctuaries and offshore island reserves, where numbers are increasing. The kokako produces the most haunting and beautiful song of all New Zealand's native birds.*

Chapter 5

PALEOGENE SEAS AND SEASHORES

65–26 million years ago

THROUGH MUCH OF THE PALEOGENE period, Zealandia continued to sink, as it had been doing ever since rifting from Gondwana. It was at its 'most drowned' during the Oligocene epoch (33.7–23.8 million years ago), at best little more than a string of islands (see maps, pages 40–1). In fact, geologists cannot be certain that Zealandia did not completely vanish beneath the waves for a period of time! (Though this would, of course, mean that all of New Zealand's dry-land plants and animals of Gondwanan origins would have had to recolonise the land mass once it had re-emerged; a far-fetched idea.) New Zealand began to rise, or re-emerge, depending on what you believe, at the start of the following epoch (the Miocene), when the boundary between the Australian and Pacific plates shifted and provoked a period of intense tectonic activity and uplift.

Back at the beginning of the Paleogene, Zealandia enjoyed a subtropical climate. When Australia and Antarctica separated 34–33 million years ago, however, Australia began to move northwards, leaving Antarctica to continue moving south to its current location over the South Pole. There, isolated and surrounded by cold circumpolar currents, the vast southern continent begin to cool. Whatever land mammals had hitched a ride upon it were doomed to frosty oblivion. And as Antarctica iced up, like some gigantic refrigerator it began to pump the cold back out again, developing the Polar Front around 10 million years ago. Chilling waters derived from the Antarctic glaciers began to spread northwards into surrounding regions of the Southern Ocean. The balmy conditions that Zealandia had enjoyed at the beginning of the Paleogene became steadily cooler as seawater temperatures dropped (they stand at little more than 7°C today).

Food, glorious food chain

Antarctica, meanwhile, hit a period of extreme productivity, which continues today. Nutrients – in particular, high levels of phosphates and nitrates – derived from volcanic activity found their way into the Southern Ocean. The constant upwelling of nutrients from great depths, the oxygen-rich cold water, and the near-constant summer sunlight combined to create the base of a rich food chain. At the bottom of the chain are the phytoplankton, billions of tiny organisms such as microscopic algae and multi-celled plants which float freely in the upper regions of the ocean. At depths of less than 200 metres the water is sufficiently

Opposite: The world's largest penguin species? The fossilised bones of this giant remained undiscovered for more than 40 million years until recently found by schoolchildren on the shore of the North Island's Kawhia Harbour. Illustrated to show its height are two of today's blue penguins – the world's smallest. Gliding overhead are flocks of false-toothed pelicans, equipped with long serrated bills for plucking fish from surface waters. Their four-toed feet had webbing between all toes like modern gannets and shags.

Above: Krill are small crustaceans with a big role to play in zooplankton. They occur in all of the world's oceans, and are an important food for baleen whales and other marine animals and seabirds. Each year whales eat half the total living weight of the Antarctic krill (Euphausia superba) *... which amounts to several million tonnes.*

clear and sunlit to allow the plants to manufacture food by photosynthesis.

The next link in the food chain is the zooplankton, a 'soup' of tiny animals ranging from the larvae of larger animals such as snails, squid, crabs, lobsters, fish, jellyfish and sea stars to adult forms of marine invertebrates. The most significant member of the Antarctic zooplankton is the krill: a reddish-pink crustacean some 5 centimetres long. A lone krill does not cut much of a dash, but these animals swarm in vast numbers, forming a food resource so bountiful that they are the heart of the entire Antarctic food chain: on the menu of baleen whales, seals, seabirds, fish and squid. During daylight hours krill mass at ocean depths of about 100 metres, where they are safe from their major predators, only rising to the surface at night to feed on smaller plankton.

The explosive evolution of planktonic life in the southern oceans, a phenomenon that is unique to the Cenozoic era (65 million years ago to the present), saw a rapid expansion in the development of other forms of marine life. The seas around New Zealand were witness to the evolution of penguins, seabirds, dolphins, porpoises and whales. With the extinction of the large marine reptiles at the end of the Cretaceous, these new marine animals soon began to exploit the niches that had been left vacant.

And with Zealandia at its greatest submergence during the Oligocene, the shallow, nutrient-rich seas surrounding the archipelago would have been teeming with marine life forms. This is known from the thick deposits of limestone (itself formed from skeletons of organisms) bearing fossils of everything from plankton to molluscs, crustaceans, echinoderms, fish, birds and cetaceans.

By 65 million years ago the ancestors of today's shorebirds had begun to appear: birds such as the now-extinct false-toothed pelicans, which hunted by catching fish, probably by scooping them up from the surface of the sea. They had bony tooth-like projections along the sides of their bills, and could swallow reasonably large fish by unhinging their lower jaws. Their wingspan was enormous, possibly more than 5 metres (compare this with the 3.5-metre span of a modern albatross!), and they probably glided rather than flew.

The first penguins

Penguins evolved from flying birds, and their wings became short and stiff, enabling them eventually to 'fly' under water. Their feathers, too, are short and densely packed with great water resistance. Some of the early penguins were huge. A few fossil bones of a giant penguin were discovered in Oamaru by Charles Traill in 1872, and are today kept at the Museum of New Zealand Te Papa Tongarewa in Wellington. Well over a century later came a spectacular find to match this. On the shores of Kawhia Harbour in 2006, children on a fossil hunt under the leadership of guide Chris Templer discovered the remains of what has proved to be one of the world's largest penguins. This bird is probably 40 million years old, placing it in the Oligocene epoch, and it would have been around the same size as Traill's penguin, standing about 1.5 metres tall and weighing a whopping 100 kilograms. As the original newspaper report put it, the bird would have 'looked some men in the eye'.

Penguins were not the only seabirds that evolved with an ability to 'fly' under water. Two species of today's diving petrels found in New Zealand's seas constantly use their wings while diving to chase and catch small fish.

These diving birds would have shared the waters with early cetaceans. *Kentriodon*, found in seas worldwide during the late Oligocene and Miocene, looked much like a modern porpoise, and, like porpoises and dolphins today, is believed to have used echolocation to communicate and hunt. The melon organ inside the head focused ultrasonic squeaks onto schools of fish, stunning or possibly even killing them.

What did Zealandia look like at this time? The distinguished palaeontologist and research scientist Graeme Stevens said in his book *Prehistoric New Zealand*, 'It defies the imagination and, indeed, when we look around for a modern equivalent of what the Oligocene land may have looked like we are hard pressed.' It may have resembled something like the Florida or Bahama quays, but in truth it is anybody's guess, and illustrators must make their interpretations based on native flora and fauna they knew existed at that time.

Left: At up to 3.6 metres, the southern royal albatross (Diomedea epomophora) *has the largest wingspan of any species of albatross. It probably evolved from an extinct New Zealand albatross species,* Manu antiquus, *that inhabited the seas around the South Island and was likely to have been a similar size.*

Chapter 6

BENEATH PALEOGENE AND NEOGENE SEAS

65–16 million years ago

Opposite: Super-jaws – an encounter between the megalodon shark and an early baleen whale. At up to 21 metres long, this worldwide shark of the late Neogene was probably the largest predatory fish ever to have lived. Megalodon would have preyed on fish, seals, dolphins and whales.

CETACEANS (THE WHALES AND DOLPHINS) are masters of their marine environment: ocean-wandering creatures measuring, in the case of the blue whale, up to 30 metres in length and 130 tonnes in weight. They have excellent hydrodynamic and thermal adaptations enabling them to swim, dive and feed in all of the world's oceans, from tropical to polar. So it is extraordinary to consider that they evolved from four-footed mammals that lived on land well over 60 million years ago during the Paleogene. Some of the tell-tale clues to their land origins lie in the skeletal details of their limbs, and in the fact that they must return to the surface after diving in order to breathe.

Certain aspects of modern cetaceans' teeth led scientists to suppose that they evolved from the mesonychids, extinct four-footed mammals with hooves. Mesonychids arose in the early Paleogene, and by 40–35 million years ago included such extraordinary examples as *Andrewsarchus*, a huge wolf-like carnivore. At 5.5 metres long, and taller than a man, this fearsome predator was possibly one of the largest mammalian land carnivores ever. *Andrewsarchus* survived by scavenging along rivers and seashores, eating washed-up carcasses. Its powerful jaws enabled it to bite through bone and shell. *Andrewsarchus* is only known from one 40-million-year-old fossil found in Asia.

Today, though, following DNA analysis, it is generally believed that cetaceans share a common ancestry with hippopotamuses and other even-toed hoofed mammals. The earliest cetacean fossils, dating back 50–60 million years, have been found in Pakistan, and include *Pakicetus*, a thickset swimming mammal with long toothed jaws, stout forelimbs and a spindle-shaped torso and tapering tail. They indicate that cetaceans evolved from hoofed animals which probably spent time feeding in plankton-rich coastal waters, eventually venturing out to sea and returning to a completely marine habitat. The pace of change in early whales was rapid. By around 46 million years ago there were transitional creatures like *Rhodhocetus* (also from Pakistan), which had four legs for land locomotion but also swam with up-and-down undulations of its long tail, powered by an increasingly flexible spine. By late Eocene times – that is, within the space of around 10 million years – truly whale-like forms had appeared and Zealandian oceans were populated by the ancestors of modern cetaceans: toothed whales, baleen whales, dolphins and porpoises.

Sharing the waters were, of course, myriad fishes, including ancestors of all three major groups: teleosts (bony fishes), elasmobranchs (sharks, rays and skates), and – most ancient of all – agnathans (jawless fishes, such as hagfish). The jawless fishes first appeared over half a billion years ago in the Cambrian period, with the sharks showing up around 100 million years later. This chapter looks at some of the most spectacular cetaceans and sharks that are known to have populated Zealandian and, later, New Zealand waters.

Basilosaurus

Between 36 and 45 million years ago, Zealandian seas were home to what was probably the largest predator of that time, the first of the giant whales named by scientists: *Basilosaurus*. Certain features of this great cetacean make it remarkable. Although it had teeth, it did not have blubber. Nor did it have a blowhole on the top of the head, and only by lifting its mouth clear of the water was *Basilosaurus* able to breathe. Time spent under the water was limited to how long it could hold its breath. (Rear-facing cranial blowholes in all cetaceans evolved much later in time.)

At up to 21 metres in length, *Basilosaurus* was a long, slender predator with large jaws and a mouth full of huge teeth, and it would have had no trouble in catching a 2-metre shark. It probably led a rather lonely life because it lacked a melon – the mass of jelly-like material in the head of modern cetaceans that focuses and emits sound pulses. (Individuals use the melon not only for navigation but also to communicate with one another, sometimes across hundreds of kilometres of ocean.) New Zealand fossil finds of *Basilosaurus* suggest that this early whale may not have had large deposits of fat, which meant that it would only have visited in summer when the waters were warmer. Perhaps *Basilosaurus'* most surprising feature was its limbs. Whereas the forelimbs had evolved into fairly typical cetacean flippers, the two hind limbs still had tiny toes. The hind limbs were probably used by both male and female for clasping one another in the mating act; obviously, this animal did not come out onto the land.

Ancient sawsharks

Among the odd-looking fishes that swam in Paleogene and Neogene seas were the ancient sawsharks. These were true sharks, with six gill openings on each

Below: The ancient whale Basilosaurus, *whose fossil remains have been found in New Zealand, lived mainly in the warm seas of the Paleogene world. Males, which were the larger sex, could reach lengths of 21 metres.* Basilosaurus *lacked a number of features typical of modern whales. For one thing it lacked blubber, which explains why it could not survive in cold waters. And the lack of a blowhole meant the entire head had to be lifted clear of the water in order for the creature to draw breath.*

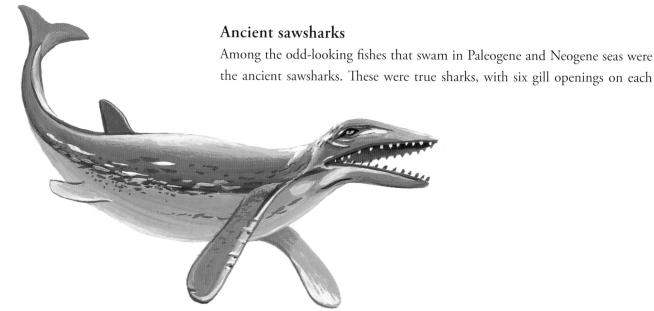

side of the head in front of the pectoral fins, but they were also equipped with a long, tooth-lined snout. Sawsharks (order Pristiophoriformes) look rather like sawfishes (order Pristiformes), and the two groups are easily confused, but there are three key points of difference. First, the sawshark has gills on the sides of the head, whereas these are beneath the head in the sawfish. Second, it has a pair of barbels (long 'feelers') below the midpoint of the snout, whereas the sawfish has none. Finally, today's sawsharks are up to 1.5 metres long while sawfishes may grow to be over 6 metres. That said, the fossils of two sawshark species indicate that these fish were twice the size of the five species of sawsharks found in New Zealand waters today. In fact, the extinct sawsharks were larger than any other sawsharks known to have existed, and lived in our waters for about 43 million years. Then as now, sawsharks cruised along the seabed, using their sensitive barbels to 'feel' prey buried in mud or sand, which they then slashed at with their snout before eating at leisure. Although sawsharks fed on crayfish, bottom-dwelling fish and shrimps, should a school of other fish pass over, the sharks would likely swim among it, slashing and killing.

A shark that killed whales

The real terror of late Neogene seas was a huge whale-killing shark that lived 16 to 1.6 million years ago. *Carcharodon megalodon* has been classified within the same genus as today's great white shark, and the two species are likely to have looked very much alike, except in one regard: size. The whale-killing shark was at least 16 metres and possibly up to 21 metres in length, and weighed at least 48 tonnes – longer and heavier than today's male sperm whale. Fossil teeth of this megalodon shark, as it is commonly called, have been found worldwide in locations that had warm seas. Its main prey were the whales and dolphins that lived offshore. Its jaws opened to more than 2 metres wide and bristled with enormous teeth growing up to 21 cm long. Like modern sharks, megalodon had several rows of teeth – top and bottom – behind the front row; if a tooth was lost during an attack, it was soon replaced. Using a tactic often employed by today's great white, megalodon would have swum into deep waters and cruised well below the surface. Upon spotting an whale or dolphin above it in the water column, megalodon would speed upwards in a vertical ascent and deliver a mammoth bite. This action had an immediate crippling effect which allowed megalodon to bite off chunks of flesh at its leisure.

About two million years ago, the world's whales moved from warmer seas where megalodon lived, into the cold waters of the Antarctic. The change of habitat roughly coincides with the extinction of this monster shark … a species loss that can only be considered good news for humankind!

Above: New Zealand's ancient endemic sawshark Ikamauius ensifer *prowled the sandy beds of Paleogene seas in search of buried animals. The fine teeth embedded in the sides of the 'saw' served as weapons for killing prey. This sawshark became extinct only 2.5 million years ago, and is survived today by eight modern species found in the Atlantic, Pacific and Indian oceans.*

Baleen whales

New Zealand fossils of ancient baleen whales show that they first began filter feeding by using their teeth some 34 million years ago. It was then that the Southern Ocean began opening up, leading to major changes in oceanic currents as well as climate change. It was a time, too, that saw the evolution of Antarctic planktonic life, which in turn became a food source for the whales. The polar ice caps developed, and the upwelling of nutrient-rich waters on the west coasts of the world's continents yielded new feeding opportunities for marine mammals. Baleen whales duly exploited this niche, evolving a filter-feeding system that could strain masses of small-bodied prey from sea water.

The evolutionary path taken by baleen whales is extraordinary: these are warm-blooded mammals, yet they feed for at least part of the year in the world's coldest oceans. The evolution of insulating blubber enabled them to hunt in icy waters, while at the same time they retained their sleek spindle shape for high-speed swimming. Fossil evidence for the evolution of baleen indicates that by 30 million years ago – that is, within the space of some four million years – filter-feeding whales already possessed toothless jaws that are structurally not unlike those of modern baleen whales.

Tusks, shark teeth and melons

New Zealand has an abundant cetacean fossil record, and some of the best finds have been made in North Otago's Waitaki River valley. This is a geologically stable area of flat land where the sea once reached 70 kilometres inland, provid-

Below: This set of maps, based upon drawings made by Charles Fleming during the 1960s, shows how the land mass was altered by changing sea levels and by tectonic activity. During the Oligocene epoch, the land underwent a 'drowning' in which it was almost fully submerged. For comparison, the outlines of the land have been placed over an outline of New Zealand today.

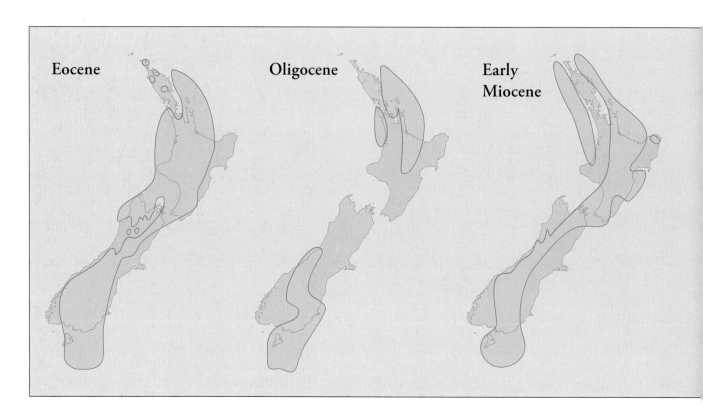

ing calm waters where ancient whales and dolphins went to breed. When these cetaceans died, they sank to the seabed and were covered in sediments that later turned to rock. Millions of years later, these rocks were lifted by tectonic activity and then eroded away, exposing the fossils. Toothed cetaceans underwent a period of rapid and wide diversification during the late Oligocene epoch. One of the most bizarre finds in New Zealand is the fossil of an ancient dolphin with a 20-centimetre tusk on its snout – looking rather like the narwhal found today in Arctic seas. The New Zealand specimen, however, appears to be related to India's Ganges River dolphins.

Another 30-million-year-old fossil find is of a squalodontid or shark-toothed dolphin that is thought to not only have lived on fish but also included penguins in its diet. Squalodontids, which became extinct some 15 million years ago, differed from today's dolphins in having a range of different tooth shapes. (A modern dolphin's teeth are uniform in shape.)

One of the key developments in cetaceans that deserves mention is echolocation, a behavioural mechanism that exploits the fact that sound travels more than five times further in water than in air. Modern whales and dolphins use a wide range of sounds to communicate, navigate and hunt prey. Echolocation among cetaceans is shown to its best effect among the toothed whales or odontocetes (which includes the dolphins, porpoises, beaked whales, sperm whale and others). *Basilosaurus* had a jawbone adapted for transmitting vibrations from the lower jaw to the middle ear, but it was not until the late Oligocene and early Miocene epochs that the melon appeared.

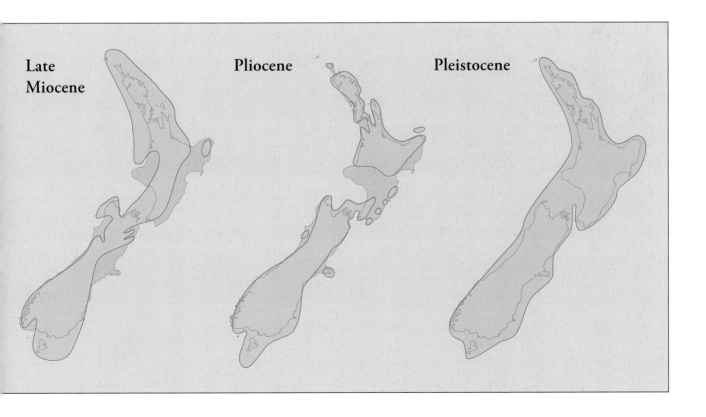

Late
Miocene

Pliocene

Pleistocene

Chapter 7

NEOGENE REPTILES, THEN AND NOW

20 million years ago to today

ONE OF THE MORE SURPRISING FOSSILS in the New Zealand fossil record is a piece of jawbone around 70 millimetres long, found near St Bathans, Central Otago, in 2006. Dating back less than 20 million years to the Neogene period, it is part of an extinct freshwater crocodile, and was discovered along with myriad other bones from a range of different creatures, including birds, fish and even what appear to be a strange mouse-like mammal and a python-like snake.

But just how surprising is it to find a crocodile in New Zealand? Australia is home to a couple of crocodile species, and one of them, the saltwater crocodile or 'saltie' (*Crocodylus porosus*), is quite capable of swimming more than 1,000 kilometres by sea, and today is found as far west as India. It has been recorded as far east as the Micronesian island of Pohnpei, which lies 4,800 kilometres north of New Zealand. Clearly, crocodiles are adept colonists.

New Zealand's crocodile would have measured 3–5 metres in length, and, judging from the location of similar fossils found around the Pacific, it thrived in either salt or fresh water. It was one of a carnivorous group known as the mekosuchines, all of which are now extinct. Their remains have also been found in Australia, New Caledonia, Vanuatu, New Caledonia and Fiji. When they arrived in New Zealand is not known, and whether they reached other island groups in the South Pacific has yet to be confirmed.

Lethal ambush

The New Zealand mekosuchine crocodile probably lived in rivers, lakes and wetland pools, also venturing onto dry land. Its diet would have included wetland birds, insects and especially fish (which make up about 70 per cent of the diet of living crocodiles and their relatives, the alligators and gavials). But it would also have attacked any moa that strayed too close to the water's edge. To catch a moa, the mekosuchine would have lain fully submerged with only its nostrils breaking the surface. Crocodiles are supreme ambush predators. Their eyes are protected by a transparent 'second eyelid'; they have flaps to keep their ears dry, and a throat flap that keeps the water from flowing into their lungs – advantageous when catching and eating prey while fully submerged.

In order to drink, a moa would have had to stand with its long legs spread and its head held just above the water's surface. It is not hard to

Opposite: A mekosuchine crocodile bursts from a lake to grab a moa that has come to slake its thirst. The mekosuchines were one of several reptile groups that survived the mass extinction of 65 million years ago, even though they are today extinct. They were found across the western Pacific islands including New Zealand.

Above: the forest gecko (Hoplodactylus granulatus), sporting the spectacular camouflage that makes geckos hard to spot, despite their sometimes bright colours. Below: Smith's skink, also known as the shore skink (Oligosoma smithi), lives up to its name and is found among the rocks, driftwood and seaweed on coasts of the north-eastern North Island.

imagine the lake waters erupting when a crocodile burst out and lunged at its prey. The jaws would have snapped shut around the bird's neck. Crocodiles have interlocking teeth and extra muscle attachments in the jaw, giving a powerful bite. With claws braced against the lake bank, the weighty crocodile could easily have tugged the moa back into deeper water, then thrashed its body violently to rip off pieces of flesh. (Crocodiles do not chew their food, but bolt it down in chunks. Like dinosaurs and moa, they swallow stones, which remain in the stomach; known as gastroliths, the stones help grind the swallowed food to make it digestible.)

The crocodilians evolved during the late Permian and early Triassic periods from the archosaurs or 'ruling reptiles', a group that also included the pterosaurs, dinosaurs and, later, birds. During the course of their 220-million-year history the crocodilians were remarkably successful, spreading worldwide and evolving into many varied forms. These even included a group of fully marine crocodiles that lived during the Jurassic and swam with the aid of a fin-like tail and paddle-like limbs. The eight genera of living crocodiles represent just a fraction of the wondrous diversity of their ancestors.

Clutch control

One interesting aspect of crocodile biology is the way in which breeding is regulated by the temperature of the surroundings. When a female is ready to lay her eggs, she finds some sandy high ground. There she spends a night first digging a hole with her hind feet, then laying a clutch of 10 to 90 eggs, which she covers with loose soil and plant material. The eggs take about 90 days to hatch, during which time the female guards the site, fiercely fending off anything – or anyone – who strays too close. Meanwhile, the plant material rots and gives off heat, keeping the clutch at a constant warmth. Should the temperature rise even further, males hatch from her eggs; however, should the temperature drop too low, the eggs produce females. This same situation applies to the native tuatara.

A foot in the past

The two species of tuatara belong to the lepidosaurs, a reptile group that also includes the lizards and snakes and is a little older than the archosaurs. Sometimes referred to as 'living fossils', tuatara are the sole survivors from a group of ancient reptiles whose fossils have been found in Europe and North America.

Left: Before the arrival of mammalian predators, tuatara were found throughout New Zealand. These are the most ancient living reptiles, having scarcely evolved since their ancestors shared the land with dinosaurs – which they predate. Given a habitat free from predators, they may enjoy a life expectancy of a century or so.

Today tuatara survive mainly on a few offshore islands around Cook Strait and the North Island. In 2005 they were reintroduced to the mainland at Karori Wildlife Sanctuary in Wellington.

Unlike crocodiles, the female tuatara makes for a rather careless mother. After picking a spot on high ground, and laying her 50 or so soft-shelled eggs, she covers them up and leaves, never to return to check on the eggs or assist the young once they emerge from their nesting chamber a year or so later, each one a perfect tiny replica of the adult.

Lizards

Also living on New Zealand's islands during the Neogene period were the ancestors of native skinks and geckos. These lizards have existed here for at least 40 million years and have evolved into more than 90 species; they occupy an extensive range of habitats, from the forest floor and canopy to the subalpine zone, scree slopes and tussock fields. Many of New Zealand's lizards are useful plant pollinators. Skinks can be found on the seashore among the seaweed and in rock cracks. Three of the species live on shores, and readily dive into sea water to either forage for food or hide from predators.

New Zealand geckos are among the oldest in the world and fall into two main groups. Geckos of the grey/green *Hoplodactylus* genus are night hunters, while those of the genus *Naultinus* live among shrubbery foliage on a diet of insects and berries. Geckos range greatly in size. Until at least the late nineteenth century, New Zealand was home to what was thought to be the world's largest gecko, the kawekaweau (*Hoplodactylus delcourti*), which grew to at least 620 millimetres long, whereas the pygmy gecko is small enough to perch on a fingertip.

Unfortunately, skink numbers have declined dramatically since the arrival of humans, and only on predator-free offshore islands does one realise what huge numbers of reptiles once thrived in this land.

Chapter 8

New Zealand's Moa

83 million to 300 years ago

MOA WERE FABULOUS BIRDS, with an ancestry that extended back in time possibly beyond the separation of Zealandia. After the extinction of Cretaceous dinosaurs and Neogene crocodiles, moa flourished to the point where they were the dominant animals in the land. It is tragic, though not surprising, that these giant birds were hunted to extinction after the arrival of Maori, who targeted them for their food and feathers, and also their bones (which were fashioned into ornaments and implements). The last moa was probably killed about two or three centuries ago and it is doubtful that a European ever set eyes on one.

How many species were there? Therein lies a tale. Europeans first discovered moa bones in 1837. In 1891, 23 species had been listed. In 1907 the tally stood at over 30; by 1949 it was back to 28. In 1991, Auckland Museum's Brian Gill acknowledged 11 species. More recently, Professor David Lambert of Massey University and his team used DNA testing to arrive at a total of nine, which is supported by Alan Tennyson in his 2006 book *Extinct Birds of New Zealand*. Tennyson notes that 'the species form three distinct groups: the two tall slender giant moa; the small athletic, alpine upland moa and the other six, which were generally more robustly built'. The nine species are shown on pages 48 to 51. Not illustrated is the coastal moa, which is described by Brian Gill in *New Zealand's Extinct Birds* and is still listed by some scientists as a tenth species.

Science has also illuminated some extraordinary details. According to DNA testing, the tallest birds in the genus *Dinornis* were all females; male birds were about half the female's size. Small fossil skeletons of *Dinornis* moa, originally thought to number three species, have now been reclassified as the male partners of the North Island giant moa (*D. novaezealandiae*) and South Island giant moa (*D. robustus*). How they managed to mate is anyone's guess! Interestingly, Professor Allan Baker from the Royal Ontario Museum and the University of Toronto, and Dr Craig Millar from the Allan Wilson Centre and the University of Auckland, more recently suggested that there may be further species. On this decision, the jury is still out.

Where did they come from?

A certain amount of mystery surrounds the origins of moa. The oldest moa fossils so far discovered are eggshell fragments only; they date from the up-

Opposite: The world's largest eagle tackles the world's tallest bird! In the space of just one million years, Haast's eagle evolved from Hieraaetus morphnoides, *which is one of the world's smallest eagles and is thought to have arrived in New Zealand from New Guinea via Australia. Talon punctures have been found in the backbones of moa fossils, suggesting that Haast's eagle did prey on the larger moa species.*

Little bush moa (*Anomalopteryx didiformis*)

This small moa was the height of a black swan. Fossils, uncovered mainly in closed-canopy forests and along forest margins, indicate that in the North Island the little bush moa frequently lived near both the slightly smaller Mantell's moa (also called Mappin's moa) and the North Island giant moa. In the South Island, it apparently lived alongside the upland moa in the limestone landscapes of Paparoa, the West Coast, and in parts of Southland. To date there are no records from Stewart Island. Back height 1.2 metres.

Upland moa (*Megalapteryx didinus*)

This smallish moa, weighing some 30 kilograms, lived in the Southern Alps, only rarely visiting the lowlands. The subalpine herbfields and tussock lands it inhabited would have been snowed over in winter, but the upland moa had feathers down to its ankles and extremely long toes which would have been an aid when walking across snow. Like the kea, and the diminutive rock wren, this specially adapted mountain moa evolved within the past five million years. It was common in the Alps, but was probably hunted to extinction by Maori after AD 1400. Back height 1.1 metres.

Crested moa (*Pachyornis australis*)

Fossil remains of this species are rare. They include a neck and skull found in 1879 in a cave at the headwaters of South Island's Takaka River, and are now in the collection of the Museum of New Zealand Te Papa Tongarewa. A series of shallow pits along the top of the skull suggests that this bird wore a crest of feathers. Although this South Island species sometimes ranged along the foothills of the Alps, it occurred in quite large numbers inland from Nelson to the West Coast, and also along the southern coast. Back height 1.5 metres.

Mantell's moa (*Pachyornis geranoides*)

This species was formerly known as Mappin's moa; the new name was only recently created for it. Only a little taller and larger than the little bush moa, Mantell's moa was restricted to the lowland areas of the lower North Island, especially along the forest margins on both coasts. Remains have also been found in wetland areas at Waikuku Beach, south of North Cape, and also at south Taranaki and Lake Poukawa in central Hawke's Bay. All these areas are associated with sand dunes alongside wetlands. This moa was commonly hunted for food. Back height 1.2 metres.

Heavy-footed moa (*Pachyornis elephantopus*)

This bird must truly have lived up to its name. In life, its legs would have resembled small tree trunks, for although the bird was short and squat it had an extremely wide pelvis and weighed as much as 250 kilograms. It lived only in the South Island, along the east coast from the bottom of the island to about Kaikoura. Since this is the drier area of the island, the moa would have kept mainly to southern beech forest, and no doubt the sight of all that meat on the move led the heavy-footed moa to become one of the first moa species to be targeted by Maori. Back height 1.5 metres.

Eastern moa (*Emeus crassus*)

The eastern, stout-legged, coastal and possibly also upland moa all had elongate trachea (windpipes) that were used in making calls. It is tempting to think that the New Zealand forest was once a noisy place that constantly rang to the booming calls of moa. The eastern moa was found only on the South Island, its range extending to almost the top end of the island. It did not range so far inland as the heavy-footed moa, being something of a coastal species. Before the arrival of Maori, eastern moa were abundant. Adults would have defended their breeding sites and food sources, relying on a swift kick to repel threats. Back height 1.4 metres.

Stout-legged moa (*Euryapteryx gravis*)

This heavy-set moa had large legs and a broad pelvis, and a bill shape indicating that it ate softer foliage than did other moa. This was another species in which females were larger than males. Its range extended from coastal Otago across to Punakaiki, and then in a much smaller area from around Blenheim inland, and along the southern coast of the North Island and up the east coast to Cape Turnagain. Back height 1.4 metres.

per Miocene, which makes them about 15 million years old. However, New Zealand has had no contact with any land mass for over 80 million years, and as moa are the only birds ever discovered that lack any trace of wings, it is presumed their ancestors walked into New Zealand before the break from Gondwana. As New Zealand's Oligocene land mass consisted of several small islands, this was previously thought to have been when ancient native birds such as the moa speciated (evolved into separate species). Modern research suggests that speciation took place about six million years ago, a time when the climate was cooler and tectonic activity heralded the formation of mountains in both the North and South islands.

An unusual aspect of moa biology is their delayed maturity. Whereas many birds are able to breed at about 12 months, moa are thought to have waited 10 years before seeking a mate. The number of eggs the female moa laid is not known, nor her laying frequency; it is likely that she laid perhaps once every two or three years, raising one or two eggs in a large nest built roughly upon the ground. Although the eggs are enormous compared with other birds' eggs, when one considers the size of the bird, they are not so large after all. (By comparison, in relation to the adult female's size, the kiwi has the world's largest egg.)

Another interesting detail about the moa is that – like the kiwi – every species had a hind toe. All the world's other ratites (flightless birds) evolved without a fourth toe. Why this should be can only be guessed at. Possibly the other ratites evolved with a facility either for running fast to escape predators or for walking great distances in search of food; a hind toe would have slowed them down.

Moa myths and mouthfuls

In the past there was a tendency to mount moa skeletons with the neck and head held proudly aloft. However, although the giant moa grew large and was able to reach up with its long neck to forage about 3 metres above the ground, the bird's normal posture would have been not too dissimilar to that of Australian emus or cassowaries, with the head held at back height. The smallest species was scarcely larger than a swan, but no doubt had the same posture and stance – just right for skulking through thick forest.

Moa did not eat grasses as was once believed, but instead favoured seeds, leaves, fruit and twigs. Like many other leaf-eating animals, they relied on gastroliths – ingested stones, which remained in the gizzard – to grind up swallowed food. With their ancient lineage, moa evolved in tandem with New Zealand's native forests. An intriguing puzzle for botanists is why such a large number of native shrubs have either a divaricating habit (typically having small leaves and 'twiggy' branches), or, like the lancewood, pass through a juvenile leaf form which is tough and unappetising, before growing into a completely different adult sporting lush, edible foliage. This latter form is only apparent after the tree reaches a height of 3 metres – interestingly, beyond the browsing height of an adult giant moa. Fossils of a divaricate shrub have been found and dated at more than 16 million years old, so this unusual growth form could not have been the result of cold conditions experienced during the Ice Ages. The divaricating habit serves as a very effective natural defence against browsers such as moa. Due to the open growth and small leaves, it offers little sustenance. And after being browsed, the plant quickly recovers.

The largest of the moa species may have weighed more than 200 kilograms, but although they were huge, they were not invincible. Within the past million years, Haast's eagle (*Harpagornis moorei*) grew to become the largest eagle in the world, and would have had no trouble in knocking down the largest moa. Another threat to moa was soft, swampy terrain, and the remains of many have been found in such places – along with giant eagles, which evidently hoped to score an easy meal from a trapped moa.

North Island giant moa (*Dinornis novaezealandiae*)

This was the world's tallest bird, but not the heaviest. (That record belongs to the elephant bird of Madagascar.) Giant moa – especially the females (illustrated) – were tall, but they were also slender and lithe, so it is likely that they could travel far in search of food; the very long neck enabled them to browse high into the trees. Although Maori slaughtered giant moa for food, curiously no stories about this fabulous bird were handed down through the generations. Back height 2 metres (female).

South Island giant moa (*Dinornis robustus*)

This species laid an egg that was almost 4 kilograms in weight, and like the North Island giant moa, the male (illustrated) was only half the height of the female. This South Island bird was content to live in forested areas, especially on the Canterbury Plains within the shelter of beech tree forests. The safety of the forests, however, lasted only until the arrival of Maori, who set them alight in order to drive the birds into open areas. Many thousands of various moa species were slaughtered at one site at the mouth of the Waitaki River north of Dunedin – just one of many known butchering sites that have been uncovered. Back height 2 metres (female).

Chapter 9

THE RISE OF THE SOUTHERN ALPS

5 million years ago

ALONG THE WESTERN SHORE of the South Island, like an immense backbone, lies the mountain chain of the Southern Alps. It is a remarkably young chain, having begun to rise only five million years ago. This was as a result of movements at the boundary of two neighbouring tectonic plates: namely, the Pacific Plate to the east, and the Australian Plate, which lies on the western side. The former is slowly moving westward, and the latter inching northward.

North of New Zealand, along the boundary line, the margin of the Pacific Plate sinks beneath the Australian Plate in a process called subduction. This has created mountains in the North Island section of the Australian Plate, lifted to their present height due to pressures in the land. To the east of the North Island the crustal material of the Pacific Plate is being forced deep below Earth's surface where it eventually melts to become magma. Because of the extreme pressures that exist at this depth, magma is periodically forced back to the surface through fissures in the overlying rock. This process results in volcanic eruptions at the Earth's surface – especially within the Taupo Volcanic Zone.

Collision and erosion

Where the plate boundary dissects the western side of the South Island, it is known as the Alpine Fault. Orbiting satellite cameras have recorded the faultline as one of the longest and straightest lines on the planet's surface. This enormous fault was created 25–30 million years ago, not by subduction but by collision. Here in the south the margins of the two great plates are not only pushing hard against each other but are actually sliding past one other. The greatest tectonic pressure occurs in the centre of the South Island, and this is where our tallest mountains are found – namely, Mount Cook or Aoraki, which rises to 3,754 metres, and Mount Tasman at 3,497 metres – in a zone of maximum uplift. There are 16 other peaks in this range that exceed 3,000 metres in height.

Although tectonic forces continue to push the crustal material of the two plates up to raise the mountains, erosion – caused by rain, rivers, glaciers and earthquakes – wears away the uplifted rocks at virtually the same rate; this can be as much as 10 millimetres a year. Since the Alps began rising five million years ago, the total rate of uplift has been over 20 kilometres. So the rocks at the summit of Mount Cook were lying below sea level only one million years ago.

Opposite: In the brief five million years over which the Southern Alps took shape, new alpine plant and animal species evolved. Three such were the upland moa, which had fully feathered legs for warmth and long toes for walking across snow; the world's only alpine parrot, the kea; and the rock wren. Plants of the alps include, clockwise from left, South Island edelweiss (Leucogenes grandiceps), *large mountain daisy* (Celmisia semicordata), *snow tussock* (Chionochloa pallens), *korikori* (Ranunculus insignis) *and giant buttercup* (Ranunculus lyallii).

Mount Cook and many of the mountains of the Southern Alps are composed of a metamorphosed sedimentary rock called greywacke and/or schist, which is made of sandstone and mudstone and is sometimes called the 'basement rock' of New Zealand. The unstable greywacke was laid down under the sea 220–200 million years ago; however, the rock of Mount Cook has been forced upwards very rapidly, geologically speaking. On 14 December 1991, the top 10 metres of the summit of Mount Cook suddenly toppled. It was widely suspected that an earthquake triggered the rock fall, but seismographs bore no record of quakes, and the avalanche was instead a result of the instability of the area. It was later estimated that the avalanche plummeted at up to 200 kilometres an hour. The rock fall happened at midnight, and fortunately no one was hurt.

Wet west winds

The 600-kilometre-long Southern Alps have a profound effect on New Zealand's weather. They present a barrier to prevailing moisture-laden westerlies that continually blow across the Tasman Sea. Known as the 'West Wind Drift', these winds encircle the southern hemisphere, and when they meet the Alps they are forced up and over the summits. The rising air cools rapidly, causing moisture to condense out of the winds; this falls as torrential rain and snow on the West Coast, nourishing the rainforests, wetlands and glaciers below. Milford Sound has at least 6,000 millimetres of rain each year. Whataroa, further north, receives an annual drenching of 15,000 millimetres, making it one of the wettest places on Earth. Interestingly, only a few kilometres away Central Otago lies within the rain-shadow on the eastern flanks, and the annual rainfall here is a mere 350 millimetres, making this the driest area in the country.

The rapid rise of the Southern Alps has had a dramatic effect on the native flora and fauna: only within the last five million years has this land been lifted high enough to have an alpine zone. This leaves us with a paradox: where, then, did our alpine species of flora and fauna come from?

Regarding the origin of endemic alpine plants, Leonard Cockayne, founder of Wellington's Otari Native Plant Museum, in 1928 stated that New Zealand's alpine plants were the results of evolutionary influences which took place over a long period of time. Eighty or so years ago, however, he would not have been aware of the young age of our mountains. In 1973 while on sabbatical in New Zealand, Dr Peter Raven, director of the Missouri Botanical Gardens, suggested that our alpine plants arrived within the past five million years and had originated from northern hemisphere relatives that had spread from mountains in the Asian and New Guinea tropics. This theory has been proved to be only partially correct, for molecular studies have shown that although approximately half of New Zealand's alpine plants have northern hemisphere relatives, many others have links with South American alpine plants, and that speciation was both recent and rapid.

Above: New Zealand's black alpine cicada (Maoricicada nigra) *is the world's only known alpine cicada, and it is truly black. The colour absorbs heat and enables the insect to warm up quickly in brief patches of sunlight that splash the peaks between passing clouds. Cicadas are classed as true bugs, with piercing and sucking mouthparts; most species are found throughout the warmer areas of the world, particularly in the tropics.*

Unique alpine animals …

Among New Zealand's habitats, none holds such a rich diversity of fauna and flora as the alpine zone. More than 90 per cent of the country's alpine plants are endemic, yet these plants simply did not exist more than five million years ago. The case is similar for several native bird species that are found only in the alpine regions, namely, the upland moa, kea and the rock wren; there is no evidence that these species existed before the rise of the Southern Alps.

Alan Tennyson in *Extinct Birds of New Zealand* states that the upland moa was the only moa species that lived in the Southern Alps, and was 'strikingly different' from any other 'in physical build, plumage and egg colour'. In *New Zealand's Extinct Birds* Brian Gill states it was also the only moa species that had feathers down to its ankles, and its feet had long toes that no doubt helped it walk through snow.

One look at the largest native bird that lives in the Southern Alps today, the kea (*Nestor notabilis*), tells you that this bird bears a marked resemblance to the native forest parrot, the kaka (*Nestor meridionalis*); it is obvious that these two birds are closely related. What is significant is that their common ancestor lived only five million years ago.

The rock wren, too, has evolved to exist in mainly alpine conditions; before the arrival of Maori, it was also an inhabitant of North Island mountains. Some gecko species have also adapted to living at an elevated altitude, and have become the world's only known alpine species. The list goes on: endemic butterflies, moths, weta and stoneflies have evolved into species that survive in alpine conditions and have been placed in unique alpine genera. In *Ghosts of Gondwana* George Gibbs states that a total of six species of giant weta and one tree weta live in the alpine zone and can survive being frozen in subzero temperatures. They are able to get up and walk away unharmed by the experience, yet they have the same body-fluid chemistry as their lowland cousins.

… and plants

Scree slopes, composed mostly of ice-fractured greywacke, occur mainly on the eastern flanks of the Alps, and are home to many unusual plants found nowhere else. Most of these are grey in colour with fleshy leaves, and have a large root system that dives through the scree to the sandy soil, which is constantly wet from water seepage. The plant with the most unusual, though appropriate, common name is the 'vegetable sheep' (*Haastia pulvinaris*). Perched high on a slope and seen from a distance, this cushion plant looks exactly like a small sheep, and more than one South Island sheepdog has been puzzled when its farmer owner has mistakenly directed it to round up a flock of cushion plants! A very beautiful alpine plant is the South Island edelweiss (*Leucogenes grandiceps*). As different a plant from a vegetable sheep as one could imagine; and yet no more than two million years ago, these two plants descended from the same ancestor.

Alpine geckos are some of New Zealand's latest gecko finds, and are very rare. They are also variable in colour, with patterns in brick-red or dull grey. Although it was originally thought that they occupied only alpine habitats above 1,000 metres, in November 2006 the Department of Conservation announced that volunteers had discovered this rare lizard in the Waitutu Forest, south-east of Fiordland.

HIGH-LIVING LICHENS

New Zealand has more than 1,000 lichen species, with at least as many more waiting to be described. Many encrust the alpine rocks, some at high altitudes. Strictly speaking, lichens are not true plants, but fungi and algae, or fungi and cyanobacteria, living in a symbiotic relationship. Pollution destroys lichens, and probably the reason New Zealand is so rich in species is because our alpine air is pollution-free.

Chapter 10

THE ICE AGES

1.8 million to 850,000 years ago

DURING THE ICE AGES THAT in New Zealand began 1.8 million years ago and ended about 850,000 years ago, the cooling of the planet's climate fluctuated considerably, producing at least 12 glacial periods interspersed with warmer periods (interglacials). From 850,000 years ago until the present time, New Zealand experienced approximately eight more ice ages. Fluctuations in temperature during the coldest part of an ice age and the warmest times of an interglacial occur slowly, and may have taken many hundreds of years to cycle. Daily temperatures were typically warm during the interglacials (that is, as warm as at present, since we are currently experiencing an interglacial), allowing kauri forests, which today occur only in the upper North Island, to flourish as far south as Wellington.

Coping in a cold climate

In the depths of an ice age, the upper third of the North Island, today the balmy location for Auckland, would have had the temperatures currently experienced in Invercargill over 1,000 kilometres to the south. Interestingly, because deep water lies between the Three Kings Islands, lying 64 kilometres north of Cape Reinga, during the ice ages these islands were never part of the main New Zealand land mass. As a consequence, they have remained completely isolated for millions of years and have developed many of their own species of flora such as the liana *Tecomanthe speciosa,* and the handsome tree *Pennantia baylisiana,* which is listed in the *Guinness Book of Records* as the world's rarest tree. Both these plants were each reduced to just one living specimen when goats were placed on the islands to feed possible shipwreck survivors.

At the height of the last ice age, which occurred about 18,000 years ago, so much of the world's supply of fresh water was trapped in ice that sea levels around New Zealand dropped by more than 120 metres, and the average temperature fell by 5°C. The effect of this was to increase New Zealand's area by 50 per cent, and the North Island, South Island, Stewart Island and many smaller islands were all part of a much larger land mass. This single island allowed native animals to roam and plants to spread over the whole of New Zealand. Auckland's Hauraki Gulf, which now has some 48 islands, consisted of a flat landscape dissected by many river valleys and dotted with hills. Foveaux Strait,

Opposite: New Zealand has experienced at least a dozen glacial periods during the past two million years or so. Between each ice age were interglacials, periods when daily temperatures warmed over many hundreds of years to produce weather conditions similar to those of today. This impression of an interglacial period in what is now Milford Sound shows the flat rocks being used as breeding colonies by the New Zealand fur seal (Arctocephalus forsteri). *During an ice age a glacier would have filled the valley to about one-third of the way up the flank of the snow-capped mountain.*

Right (left to right): Acacia, eucalyptus and casuarina are three common Australian trees that were also common in New Zealand 15 million years ago, and whole forests of any of these species could have been found throughout the land. But the ice ages of the past three million years proved too cold for their survival, and now they are found only as planted exotics.

which separates the bottom end of the South Island from Stewart Island, would likewise have been dry land, and the Bay of Islands would also have been a 'bay of hills' rising from a dry flat plain.

The cold weather killed off most of New Zealand's conifer–broadleaf forest (temperate rainforest), which by then survived only in the top quarter of what would become the North Island; in the northern hemisphere almost all temperate rainforest was eradicated during the ice ages. Native trees represent the antiquity of New Zealand's forest, which dates back to Gondwana days, and are living monuments to a bygone era.

The deepest freeze

During that last and most devastating ice age, southern beech forest grew as far north as Taranaki, in the lower third of the North Island. Further south, the forest gradually gave way to shrubs and grassland, and, finally, grassland extended down the entire east coast of the South Island, across the Canterbury Plains and into the foothills of the mountains. Vegetation consisted of low-growing plants mixed with rocks, gravels and fellfield plants. Fiordland, located at the lower end of the South Island's west coast, received a year-long blast of frigid air travelling for thousands of kilometres across the Southern Ocean. New Zealand's mild climate plunged dramatically and the Southern Alps were heaped with snow, especially down their entire western flanks. Rivers quickly froze and became slow-moving glaciers that rose up above their banks, often merging with other glaciers to become immense sheets of slow-moving ice. Valleys of solid rock were scoured out to become today's spectacular U-shaped fiords, down which the glaciers pushed and flowed out into the Tasman Sea.

During the glacial period the Southern Alps were never without their blanket of ice and snow. On their eastern flanks, vast creeping sheets of ice were also transforming the landscape; grinding out valleys to a depth that was often lower than today's sea level. After the pendulum of the last ice age swung towards the warmer atmosphere of an interglacial, the glaciers and the ice-sheets began to

Below: Strawberry fungus (Cyttaria gunnii). This southern hemisphere parasitic fungus is especially found on the native silver beech tree. A similar species of both fungus and beech tree can be found in South Australia and South America proving the ancient physical link between all three land masses.

melt, and the valleys slowly filled with fresh meltwater to become the southern lakes we know today; lakes such as Te Anau, Wanaka and Manapouri. On the western flanks, and at various altitudes from today's sea level to near the mountaintops, lakes of all sizes and kinds – tarns, kettle lakes, cirques – were left as a memento of the severe cold, their waters filling hollows scooped from the rock by the erosive power of ice. Other lakes have merely filled hanging valleys that have spawned lofty waterfalls. We can thank the ice ages for the spectacular scenery which abounds in Fiordland.

Evidence of Fiordland's once enormous glaciers is not hard to find, should one take a launch trip along the majestic fiord of Milford Sound, sculpted by a frozen river of ice. The sheer walls are marked with striations: horizontal grooves gouged by rocks embedded in the ice as the glacier flowed inexorably towards the sea. The same evidence of glacial gouging can also be found on an island in Lake Manapouri.

Moving mountains

Glaciers carry rocks of all sizes from mountaintops down into lowland areas. Where the glaciers ended – some inland, some at the coasts – the ice rapidly melted and the rocks and boulders were dropped in huge piles called moraines. On the South Island's west coast, moraines form small hills and ridges, some of which run for many kilometres. Today, these ridges often run right into the sea itself (now at a level many metres higher). On the eastern side of the main divide, glaciers transported rocks and gravel, contributing to the building of the Canterbury Plains, although most of this construction work was accomplished by the many braided rivers that flow eastward from the Southern Alps, their main flows dividing along the way into hundreds of smaller streams that twist and turn, join and rejoin. Braided rivers are fairly rare, and the Canterbury Plains have some of the finest examples in the world.

New Zealand's last ice age is believed to have been the coldest of them all, and wrought the most extreme changes on the landscape, on account of the forest-killing cold in the north and vast ice sheets and glaciers in the south.

The arrival of the ice ages led to the northward migration of most, if not all, non-hardy animals and plants, but this was not enough for warmth-loving plants such as casuarina and eucalyptus, which were killed off by the cold. Seals, sea lions and penguins likewise migrated northwards during the ice ages, then retreated southwards again during the interglacials. At the height of the ice age, southern beech forests were hemmed into sheltered valleys, and podocarp and kauri forest survived no further south than the Auckland isthmus. The rest of the country – with the exception of the areas locked in snow and ice – was truly barren, with large areas of subalpine and alpine meadows. How many plants and animals, unable to adapt or to head north, succumbed to the big chill, may never be known.

Above: Umbrella fern (Sticherus cunninghamii), *and below, horopito* (Pseudowintera colorata) *– just two of several plants whose ancestry dates back to the ancient continent of Gondwana. They have survived geological upheaval, Oligocene 'drowning' and Pliocene ice ages.*

Chapter 11

TAUPO ERUPTS

1,800 years ago

LYING AT THE HEART OF THE VOLCANIC PLATEAU and covering an area almost equal in size to the island of Singapore, Taupo is the largest lake in either Australia or New Zealand (if one excludes the dry Lake Eyre in South Australia). It has a perimeter of 193 kilometres and a surface area of 616 square kilometres, and is 186 metres deep at its deepest point. Today Taupo is a popular recreational area that in summer is the home of water-sports and boating attractions. The lake is amply stocked with trout, and the scenic perimeter road is the setting for annual sporting events. The houses and cottages lining the shores change hands for big sums. In winter the highly active Mount Ruapehu volcano at the lake's southern end provides a playground for skiers. Two further active volcanoes, Tongariro and the young cone of Ngauruhoe, are located close by.

Peaceful scenes like these can mask the sobering fact that Lake Taupo is in fact a caldera: a volcanic collapse structure formed by the rapid eruption of a magma chamber. And according to the United States Geological Survey, it is the third-largest caldera in the world.

A violent history

Taupo's volcanic history goes back at least a quarter of a million years. The caldera was formed as a result of a cataclysmic volcanic eruption that ejected well over 1,800 cubic kilometres of volcanic debris. The volcano has undergone at least 28 eruptions in the last 26,500 years. The most recent of these, which occurred 1,800 years ago, created a column of volcanic mud, ash and pumice that rose almost 50 kilometres into the air – which is as high into the atmosphere that an eruption column can theoretically travel, and is twice the height of the eruption column generated in 1980 by Mount St Helens in Alaska.

Moreover, Taupo is far from dead; it is merely sleeping, for it is the world's most frequently active rhyolite volcano. Its AD 181 eruption caused the loudest explosion known on Earth in the past 5,000 years, and generated ash clouds that affected Europe and China's weather for many years, recorded as 'the years of the golden sunsets'. That more eruptions are to come is not in doubt.

Although most volcanoes such as Mount St Helens, Japan's Mount Fuji or New Zealand's Mount Taranaki (which volcanologists are sure will erupt again within the next 50 years) build tall cones, some volcanoes are so explosive that

Opposite: Taupo has erupted many times. During the most recent eruption, which took place 1,800 years ago, a large forest surrounding the lake was home to thousands of birds. With the exception of the red-crowned parakeet (flying past the moa), the kingfisher and the New Zealand scaup, all other birds portrayed – including the North Island takahe (foreground, centre) – were hunted to extinction by pre-European Maori. Also illustrated is the world's largest gecko, the kawekaweau (Hoplodactylus delcourti), now extinct.

they create huge collapse structures, the calderas eventually filling with rainwater. Taupo's magma is silica-rich rhyolite that erupts explosively, mainly as pumice and ash, which is now spread across the countryside.

Before Taupo's eruption of 1,800 years ago, a large native forest surrounded the lake; forest that would have been home to many thousands of moa and other flightless birds such as the adzebill and the North Island takahe. Flighted birds would have included wrens, piopio and whiteheads. Their sanctuary would only ever have been disturbed by avian raptors, including the giant Haast's eagle.

The eruption, thought to have taken place in late summer, when bird life was profuse among the fruit-laden trees of the forest, is likely to have begun with a swarm of small but ground-shaking earthquakes over the course of several weeks. It is tempting to speculate on whether the birds heeded these warnings; quite probably, the shakes caused no more than a passing disturbance. Animals do, however, seem to have a 'sixth sense' when it comes to sensing earthquakes, and it is equally possible that by the time the volcano erupted, they had fled.

Following the quakes, the next eruption phase began beneath the waters of the lake with a series of explosions. As the red-hot magma mixed with the lake water, plumes of geysers burst from the surface, rising high into the air and giving off noxious, sulphurous fumes. The eruptive phase rapidly intensified, and the pressure of the magma beneath the lake raised the volcano's main vent above the water's surface. The roar from the main vent would have been deafening and caused any remaining birds to take wing (or run!). Pumice was blown high into the air only to fall over a wide area, showering the bird life, of which perhaps only the ground-dwellers might have survived on account of the trees that shielded them from some of the lethal downpour. Clouds of superheated steam resulting from lake water pouring into the volcano's throat would have clouded the lake's surface, drifting across the water like a dense fog.

Taupo explodes

There then followed what was possibly the most violent phase: a devastating explosion. Whether it came within weeks, days or hours of the previous phase is not known, but it was sudden. And when it did, a column of ejecta towered into the sky, then collapsed under gravity to generate a pyroclastic flow (see panel, left) that sped away from the vent at speeds of up to 900 kilometres per hour.

In a *National Geographic* magazine article on the history of the world's volcanoes, Taupo's AD 181 eruption was listed as being 100 times greater than the eruption of Mount St Helens. The pyroclastic hurricane that it unleashed can be seen today as a pinkish layer of volcanic material within the walls of road cuttings, and also near the top of ocean cliffs eroded by the sea. (A layer of ignimbrite from this eruption can be seen near the clifftops close to the mouth of the Waikato River – some 180 kilometres from the vent of the volcano.) Scientists estimate that over 100 million tonnes of pumice was released each second

PYROCLASTIC FLOWS

A pyroclastic flow is a cloud of superheated volcanic dust and pumice that flows downhill under the pull of gravity, often at very high speed. The historic eruption of Italy's Mt Vesuvius in ad 79 produced a pyroclastic flow that buried the Roman town of Pompeii and killed more than 2,000 residents. In later eruptions of Vesuvius in ad 47 and 1631, pyroclastic flows killed over 4,000 people, destroyed 15 villages and covered Naples with 45 centimetres of ash. Extraordinary film footage of a huge pyroclastic flow was captured in 1980, when Mt St Helens exploded into life with a force equal to 27,000 Hiroshima atomic blasts. Despite the many warning earthquakes, 57 people were killed within the volcano's shadow. An estimated 1,500 elk, 5,000 deer and 11 million fish perished, along with untold numbers of birds.

during this most eruptive phase. Pumice from the eruption can still be gathered from beaches on the North Island's west coast.

The devastation would have been total over a wide radius throughout the forests surrounding Lake Taupo. Even with several days' head start, the native birds would have been outrun by the wall of heat. At least 20,000 square kilometres of the central North Island were laid waste by hot ash and pumice, along with thousands of hectares of rainforest, some of which may have dated from the end of the last ice age 8,000 years previously. Millions of trees were either tossed like matchsticks or incinerated outright: trees that were home to insects, skinks, geckos and tuatara, whose only means of defence was to either stay stock-still, or burrow deeper into their excavated homes in the trees' timbers.

Pouakani totara: a majestic monument

Despite the devastation, no more than 20 kilometres from the volcano's vent, pockets of forest which lay in the lee of hills actually survived. And in one such pocket, a totara seed fell into a thick layer of volcanic ash and mud, sprouted,

Below: At 42.7 metres tall and at an estimated 1,800 years old, the giant Pouakani totara (Podocarpus totara) is the tallest and oldest totara tree in the land. The tree grows in a private reserve, near Mangapehi in the North Island's King Country, and as its age indicates, it began growing immediately after the last great eruption of Lake Taupo 1,800 years ago.

and began to grow. Over a thousand years later, Maori arrived in the North Island. When they eventually located this huge tree they called it Pouakani, and declared the living monument to be tapu, or sacred. To gaze up at this giant, the tallest and most ancient totara tree in New Zealand, is to step back 1,800 years in time.

Earlier this century a bulldozer unearthed a number of ancient podocarp trees that had been flattened by the Taupo eruption, then buried in ash and mud. The timber of the blasted trees was as fresh as if it had been felled only yesterday. The find created barely a ripple in the conservation world, which is remarkable when one considers that along with these entombed trees may come treasures for modern science: specimens of moa, perhaps, preserved beneath the ash and mud. If such specimens are found they would amount to a significant discovery. Could it be that the North Island has its very own 'Pompeii' right alongside Lake Taupo?

Chapter 12

AUCKLAND'S VOLCANOES

150,000 to 600 years ago

WITH OVER 1.4 MILLION RESIDENTS, Auckland is New Zealand's largest city by far. One of its most distinctive features is the large number of small steep hills that stud the low, rolling terrain of the isthmus across which the city sprawls. The hills are extinct volcanoes – 49 of them in all. Some eruptions resulted in volcanic cones, while lesser eruptions produced rings of small hills that have been eroded to become either lakes filled with fresh water, or lagoons breached by the sea.

Auckland's volcanic history probably began 150,000 years ago; however, the latest eruption occurred a mere 600 years ago, and was the only occasion when a sequence of volcanic activity in Auckland was witnessed by humans. This eruption resulted in the building of the largest cone in the Auckland field, the island of Rangitoto, which rises from the sea to 260 metres, about twice the altitude of any of the other volcanoes in the field.

Warming up

Auckland's volcanic activity is for the most part 'monogenetic', meaning that each volcanic centre relates to a single eruption. (An exception to this rule is Panmure Basin, where geologists from GNS and the University of Auckland discovered a 'volcano within a volcano' during field research in February 2008.) The field is far from extinct, and if we look at the frequency of eruptions over the past several millennia, a rather disturbing trend appears. There were at least nine eruptions in the first 50,000 years – on average, one every 5,500 years. There were at least 21 volcanic eruptions in the Auckland field during the following 80,000 years, averaging one every 3,500 years. Then, during the past 20,000 years, there were 19 eruptions, or one every 1,000 years on average, the most recent being that of Rangitoto. Volcanoes are notoriously unpredictable, and those in Auckland appear to be getting larger, not smaller, and the frequency of eruptions may be increasing.

Hot spots

What are the origins of all this volcanism? It is all down to a large field of basaltic magma (molten basalt rock), otherwise known as a hot spot, about 100 kilometres below ground. Every 1,000 years or so, a fresh batch of basaltic magma

Opposite: South-central Auckland, more than 18,000 years ago. A female stout-legged moa (far right) and her partner are joined by a Mantell's moa (left) to watch a sudden burst of volcanic activity in Mt Mangere's main crater. Overhead two paradise shelduck flee the disturbance; the female has a white head, and the male sports a black head. A North Island weka (bottom left) stalks past, unperturbed. To the south-west of Mangere's volcanic cone lies a shallow crater that had erupted earlier. Approximately 7,000 years ago, this crater was invaded by rising sea levels and is now known as the Mangere Lagoon.

rises from the hot spot to the surface, a journey that takes several weeks. Upon reaching the surface, the magma erupts as lava. Should magma arrive at the surface and encounter a body of water – be it a river, the sea or ground water – the resulting explosion can produce a small but devastating volcanic event. This is known as a phreatomagmatic eruption, and occurs when magma of more than 1,000°C comes into contact with surface water, which is immediately turned into superheated steam. As a consequence, large quantities of steam, gas, fragmented lava and shattered rock are hurled up and away from the explosion site in a rapidly expanding circular cloud, which may be as high as 500 metres and reach speeds of several hundred kilometres per hour. More than 70 per cent of Auckland's volcanoes show signs of phreatomagmatic activity.

Some of Auckland's volcanoes are circled with a base surge that has travelled outwards from the main vent for more than 1.5 kilometres; this ring of volcanic material is known as tuff. Any future phreatomagmatic explosion resulting in a rapidly expanding base surge would cause significant loss of human life and property – and this type of eruption can occur with little warning.

Should the magma not come into contact with surface water, the volcanic activity is driven largely by gas to produce a flaming fountain of white-hot magma, a process known as fire fountaining, which then begins to build a volcanic cone. Auckland examples of this type include Mount Mangere, Mount Albert, Mount Victoria and One Tree Hill. When fire fountaining 'runs out of steam', as it were, the lava continues to flow more slowly, and, as in the case of Mount Mangere, the crater rim is breached and the lava stream continues to flow down the sides of the scoria cone. (See illustration on previous page.)

In some of Auckland's volcanic sites, however, the quantity of lava reaching the surface was so extensive that lava lakes formed, though they were usually confined within the tuff ring. Such a circular hill of shattered rock and ash formed a tuff ring around one of the city's oldest volcanoes, the site of which is now occupied by the Auckland Domain. The hospital and the Auckland War Memorial Museum have been built on opposite sides of this large tuff ring. When European settlers first arrived in the 1840s, the Domain tuff ring enclosed a large swamp where a small freshwater spring was located. This small spring became the first source of Auckland's fresh water, and later became the home of young American rainbow and brown trout, which were then released into the country's lakes and rivers. Eventually, the swamp was drained, and the resulting flat land has become home to many cricket pitches.

The eruptions begin . . .

Auckland's first eruptions occurred within what is now the heart of Auckland City, and these were followed later by eruptions to the north of the harbour, which gave rise to the explosion craters of Tank Farm, Pupuke and Onepoto, and the cones now called North Head and Mount Victoria.

Opposite: Modelled on the 1865 original by Austrian geologist Ferdinand von Hochstetter, this map of Auckland's volcanoes shows how the cones and lakes played a key role in shaping the city's distinctive landscape.

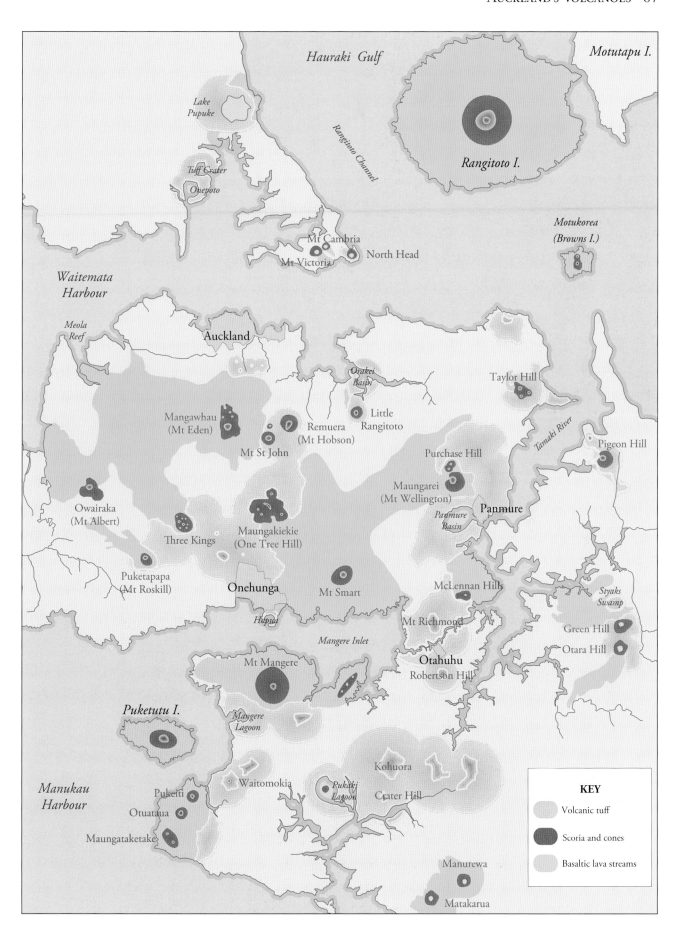

Hauraki Gulf

Motutapu I.

Lake Pupuke

Rangitoto Channel

Tuff Crater

Onepoto

Rangitoto I.

Motukorea
(Browns I.)

Mt Cambria

Mt Victoria   North Head

Waitemata
Harbour

Meola
Reef

Auckland

Orakei
Basin

Taylor Hill

Mangawhau
(Mt Eden)

Remuera
(Mt Hobson)

Little
Rangitoto

Mt St John

Tamaki River

Pigeon Hill

Purchase Hill

Maungarei
(Mt Wellington)

Panmure

Owairaka
(Mt Albert)

Three Kings

Maungakiekie
(One Tree Hill)

Panmure
Basin

Puketapapa
(Mt Roskill)

Onehunga

Mt Smart

McLennan Hills

Styaks
Swamp

Mt Richmond

Green Hill

Hupui

Otara Hill

Mangere Inlet

Otahuhu

Robertson Hill

Mt Mangere

Puketutu I.

Mangere
Lagoon

Kohuora

Manukau
Harbour

Waitomokia

Rukaki
Lagoon

Crater Hill

Pukeiti

Otuataua

KEY

Maungataketake

Volcanic tuff

Scoria and cones

Manurewa

Basaltic lava streams

Matakarua

Later eruptions resulted in the building of two large volcanic cones at Mount Albert and Mount Roskill. The former has been modified by extensive quarrying, which removed the top 15 metres. Mount Roskill was not heavily quarried, and its two craters live on as car parks. The remains of Mount Roskill's tuff ring have been incorporated into the landscape design of the Akarana Golf Course.

Fifteen kilometres to the south are the volcanic cones of Ihumatao, Papatoetoe and Wiri. These three small volcanoes represent the most southerly volcanoes in the Auckland volcanic field. Crater Hill, located a little to the north, was almost razed by quarrying in the last hundred years or so. Fortunately, the explosion crater of nearby Pukaki has escaped quarrying and is one of the best examples of this type of explosion crater.

The remaining volcanoes of South Auckland frequently had more than one cone: Mount Richmond shows evidence of extensive fire fountaining, which produced more than seven individual vents; and the nearby McLennan Hills volcano spilled so much lava that it actually dammed the upper reaches of the Manukau Harbour.

Then rose the volcanic giants: One Tree Hill; the three volcanoes of Three Kings that have been so heavily quarried by Europeans; Mount Mangere, which produced an extensive lava flow and was later buried beneath a thick layer of volcanic ash; Mount Smart; Mount Eden; Mount Wellington; and, finally, the volcano that ejected more lava that all previous eruptions – Rangitoto. The name given by Maori to Auckland's much-loved shield volcano is an abbreviation of nga rangi-i-totongia-a-tama-te-kapu, which roughly translates as 'the day of the bleeding of Tama Te Kapua'. The shortened form of Rangitoto means 'sky of blood', describing the island's fiery birth.

Motutapu, ancient Maori settlement

Rangitoto's neighbour is the volcanic island of Motutapu, one of about 48 islands that rise from the waters of Auckland's Waitemata Harbour in the Hauraki Gulf (Waitemata means 'obsidian waters', named for its glassy surface; Hauraki means 'north wind'). A maritime park was established in 1967 to preserve this 13,600 square kilometres of Pacific Ocean.

Today, the large outer islands of the Gulf are mainly used for conservation, and the inner islands for recreation. During pre-European times many of the islands, and also the hills on the slender isthmus of Auckland, came to be widely settled by Maori, who appreciated the defensive qualities of the now quiet volcanic mounds.

Exactly when Maori first settled on Motutapu is not known, but evidence suggests that several hundred individuals were living on the island 600 years ago. Motutapu is no more than 8 kilometres from the mainland to the south, 10 kilometres to the west, and about 15 kilometres from today's Auckland City. The Maori settlers would have lived in a pa (a fortified village), growing

Above: Whau tree. The Mt Eden volcano began erupting approximately 12,000 years ago, and during the last stages of the eruption, fire fountaining began in the most westerly of the volcano's three craters not long before the final discharge of lava. More than 11,000 years would pass before Maori settlers arrived to find the most common plant growing on the extinct cone, the whau tree. They consequently gave the cone its Maori name, Maungawhau, 'a mountain covered with whau trees'. The whau is thought to have the lightest timber of any tree in the world, and was used by Maori for making fishing floats.

vegetable crops such as kumara. They would have been familiar with the Auckland landscape, dotted as it was with many small 'hills'. The tallest of these, Maungawhau or Mount Eden (196 metres), was also crowned with a pa, and was home to Maori.

It is possible that the inhabitants of Motutapu received a 'warning' that a new volcano was about to be born on the western shores of their island. This warning would have come in the form of earth tremors for several days or even weeks before the initial volcanic explosion. As the new volcano rose out of the sea, quite possibly the first indication of danger was a phreatomagmatic submarine explosion, with the ensuing displacement of water creating a small tsunami.

When it finally came, Rangitoto's birth would have been extremely violent. As the basaltic magma burst through the sea floor and came in contact with the sea water, gargantuan explosions hurled large quantities of hot rock and ash high into the air, and possibly a fire fountain, too, smothering Motutapu with the ejecta. It is not known how long the initial eruption stage lasted, nor if there was more than one. Some geologists estimate that the volcano continually erupted for 10 years, while others have suggested the eruption phase may have lasted for 200 years. However long it lasted, Rangitoto produced a volume of lava roughly equal to that of all Auckland's other 48 volcanoes combined: some 2,300 million cubic metres in all.

By general standards, Auckland's cones are small; most are less than 150 metres in height. Compare this with the 2,291-metre height of Ngauruhoe in the central North Island, or with 4,392-metre Mount Rainier in Washington State, USA.

There is no record of the fate of those living on Motutapu. And exactly when Maori returned to Motutapu is not known, either; but after a heavy ash fall from Rangitoto, two adults and one child walked across an ash field before it had fully cooled. By the time all the heat generated by this ash field had dissipated, the ash had been petrified, and their footprints were recorded for all time.

Conserving the skyline

The fascinating geology of Auckland's volcanic field was not always held in high regard. Early Maori carried out extensive modifications to the tallest hills when establishing their pas, cutting down the trees that grew naturally on the slopes, and then digging extensive gardens with windbreaks to shield their vegetable crops. They had in the main deserted the cones by the time Europeans arrived to settle the Auckland isthmus. The new arrivals quarried the cones extensively for their scoria, putting it to use in building roads and walls.

Today, Auckland's unique volcanic field is enjoyed by residents and visitors alike. Several of the tallest cones have roads leading to their summits which give splendid views over the Waitemata and Manukau harbours, and also over the city and its conspicuous green cones.

Above: Pohutukawa. Many of Auckland's volcanic cones were home to this iconic New Zealand tree, whose natural range was the top third of the North Island. A large pohutukawa tree was thought to have once grown on top of the One Tree Hill volcano, as reported in one daily newspaper printed in the 1880s – although some Maori dispute this. The flanks of Rangitoto are now home to the largest forest of pohutukawa trees to be found growing anywhere in New Zealand.

Chapter 13

Lost Swamp Forests and Wetland Birds

750 years ago to today

NEW ZEALAND'S LAND MASS HAS ALMOST always been a series of many islands of various sizes surrounded by vast stretches of sea, a geological configuration that inevitably attracts offshore winds laden with billowing, moisture-laden clouds and a fairly high rainfall. Before the arrival of Polynesian settlers, these islands were clothed in temperate rainforest and endowed with extensive wetlands, particularly on the western sides of both main islands, lying as they do in the path of prevailing winds. Since the arrival of European settlers, more than 80 per cent of New Zealand's wetland area has been drained for farming.

Swamp forests, home of the kahikatea

Many of the original wetlands fringed the country's lakes, and beyond the wetlands were the swamp forests. These were forested wetlands dominated by our most ancient and tallest podocarp tree, the kahikatea (*Dacrycarpus dacrydioides*), which is also the most prominent of our few trees that can tolerate waterlogged soils. Probably no more than 2 per cent of New Zealand's original swamp forests remain today, and the largest and most spectacular of these can be found in Whirinaki Forest Park, described by Professor John Morton (in his book *To Save a Forest*) as 'one of the great forests of the world'. (A unique feature of the North Island's Whirinaki Forest is a thick foundation of volcanic material, probably a legacy of the latest eruption of the giant that currently slumbers beneath Lake Taupo.)

Swamp forests have been described as being the oldest surviving forest type on Earth. They are virtually the same today as they were millions of years ago, back in the days when dinosaurs splashed among the trees. The dinosaurs, like most reptiles, are likely to have been perfectly confident in water, many of them being strong swimmers, and no doubt they would have spent a lot of time seeking food in such areas. (Somewhat surprisingly, there were even fish-eating dinosaurs – a fact that came to light in 1983 when a 10-metre-long, 4-metre-tall fossil of a fish-eating dinosaur was found in quarry rocks in Surrey, southern England, just before bulldozers moved in. Bones and scales of a prehistoric fish were found in its stomach region. A life-size model of the dinosaur, *Baryonyx walkeri*, is on display at the National History Museum in London. Evidence of fish-eating dinosaurs has yet to be unearthed in New Zealand.)

Opposite: This scene recreates a South Island wetland of the past, stocked with birds that are now extinct. Fronting a forest of mixed southern beech and podocarp are (clockwise from background left) Finsch's duck, New Zealand stiff-tailed ducks and New Zealand swans. In the foreground, from left, are an adzebill, a pair of Finsch's ducks and a South Island flightless goose.

Some of New Zealand's swamp forests have more accurately been described as 'floating swamp forests', on account of the manner in which waterlogged areas became colonised by the seeds and seedlings of the kahikatea and other swamp forest trees. Beneath the surface of the marsh their intertwined roots have joined to form great spreading rafts. Above the surface of the swampy ground these trees have 'plank buttressed' roots (thin supporting roots around the base of the tree that divide into a network of aerial rootlets), enabling the tree to 'breathe' in the ooze. This enables kahikatea trees to grow on 'floating' platforms.

Sadly, along with the mass conversion of swamp forests into farmland, the stands of mighty kahikatea trees have been destroyed, their timber used largely for making butter-boxes in which butter was once packed and sent to England. Few mature stands of kahikatea now remain.

Other trees of the swamp forest

Not all floating swamp forests consisted entirely of kahikatea trees, for these are also the favoured growing situations of the tallest flowering plant in the land, the pukatea (*Laurelia novae-zelandiae*). These noble trees have root systems similar to the kahikatea in that they also are buttressed, and snake over the surface of the swamp. Some of the roots form solid wooden hoops that rise into the air and are called pneumatophores: 'breathing' roots which enable the tree to respire in the muddy ground. The pukatea in fact grows all over the North Island in suitable locations, and also thrives on the South Island's West Coast. It can be hard to locate in dense forest locations, but the 'plank' buttressed roots are good markers for identification, as are the fallen leaves that have 'fringed' margins, and quickly turn yellow when they fall to the ground.

In North Island swamps one can sometimes find the northern rata tree (*Metrosideros robusta*). This strange tree frequently begins life as an epiphyte, high in the branches of a host tree. As the rata tree matures, aerial roots descend the trunk of the host, and then sprawl across the ground. When the host finally dies, the rata has enough roots fused together to form a substantial 'trunk', which becomes hollow as the host tree withers away. Perhaps the most notable feature occurs in summer when the outer branches are festooned with bright crimson flowers, sometimes covering the foliage with a gorgeous floral display.

Another, smaller, forest tree that favours these growing conditions is the white-barked swamp maire (*Syzygium maire*), known to Maori as maire tawaki. This tree is found mainly in the North Island in swampy locations. It is a handsome tree from a distance; close inspection of the small leaves will reveal that they are often covered with tiny blisters, and on each stalk spidery white flowers are borne to be followed in autumn by bright red berries.

During March and April, kahikatea trees may produce masses of small fruits that are a deep purple when first formed, ripening later to a beautiful golden/red colour and quickly turning yellow when fallen. On top of each luscious fruit sits a small, round black seed, which is attractive to birds. If one assumes that kahikatea remain little changed since Cretaceous times, it is fair to assume also that the fruits must have been appealing to dinosaurs – especially since kahikatea often produce an abundant crop.

The flaxes bordering the lake in the illustration on page 71 would have grown profusely on the South Island's West Coast wetlands; along with cabbage trees, they were the first plants to colonise the glacial moraines left by the melting ice some 11,000 years ago. Flaxes provided a platform on which podocarp seeds dropped by birds germinated and began to grow.

Extinct wetland birds

The bark of swamp forest trees supports a variety of mosses and ferns, and their branches are laden with gardens of epiphytes that may also bear succulent fruits in autumn. Insects abound in such forests, and so do birds. Forest birds traditionally attracted to these swamps include the insect-eating tomtit and rifleman, fruit-eating pigeon, kokako and saddleback, and the nectar-feeding tui, bellbird and North Island stitchbird, as well as the now-extinct bush wren and huia. At ground level one may find Australasian bittern and brown teal.

The swamps were also a habitat for fishes, amphibians and reptiles, yielding another food source for birds. Many herbivorous birds, insect-eaters and fishing birds that once fed in our formerly vast wetlands were taken for food by Maori and are now extinct. A number of these are described below, and some also are featured in the illustration.

One reptile that would have posed a threat to birds until its fairly recent extinction was the mekosuchine crocodile (see Chapter 7). It was large enough to tackle moa; but, because of their weight and dietary needs, moa would have avoided wetlands and marshy areas.

South Island flightless goose (*Cnemiornis calcitrans*)

There were two distinct species of this 1-metre-tall bird: one in the North Island and another, larger species in the South Island. Both birds not only had reduced wings but the bend of each wing had a spur, rather like the spurs on the wings of Australasian spur-winged plovers. Their bones have been commonly found, so they must have been widespread and numerous in their favoured feeding grounds of wetlands and grasslands.

Finsch's duck (*Chenonetta finschi*)

This heavily built duck was once common in both the North and South islands, and its remains have been found in caves and in Maori middens. It was flightless, with much-reduced wings, but its ancestors were likely to have been strong flyers that arrived from Australia, and over a long period – perhaps 10,000 years or so – lost the power of flight.

Above: South Island flightless goose. Like its North Island counterpart, this was a big bird, at least three times heavier than one of today's Canada geese.

Above: This scene depicting the buttressed trunks of kahikatea is one of the last remaining swamp forests in New Zealand, and can be found growing around the fringes of the Arahaki Lagoon in the centre of the North Island's Whirinaki Forest Park. Swamp forests such as this flourished throughout New Zealand since the days of the dinosaur, and are sometimes referred to as 'dinosaur forests'. Most have now been drained and cleared of trees, and the land given over to cattle and deer pastures.

Stiff-tailed duck (*Oxyura vantetsi*)

New Zealand discoveries of fossil remains of *Oxyura* were made in 1983, but the species was only formally identified in 2004, by Trevor Worthy, who reviewed 13,000 waterfowl bones found at North Island's Lake Poukawa site. In his book *Extinct Birds of New Zealand*, Alan Tennyson suggests that this duck was present in the South Island, and that it may have been driven to extinction by early hunters.

South Island adzebill (*Aptornis defossor*)

There were once two species of this bird. The South Island adzebill was probably very similar to its North Island cousin, but much larger (the largest individuals possibly being slightly bigger than the smallest moa species). Its favoured habitat was open areas with little forest, and alongside wetlands; to date, fossils have not been found near the coast or in mountainous regions. The adze-like shape of the bill suggests that adzebills may have been carnivorous, and as they were completely flightless, they were probably efficient ground-dwelling predators.

Scarlett's duck (*Malacorhynchus scarletti*)

Once found in both the North and South islands as well as the Chatham Islands, Scarlett's duck was a distinctively patterned waterfowl that was almost twice the size of the Australian pink-eared duck, which shares the same genus.

Ornithologists have ascertained that because this duck had a large and unusually flat bill, it did not dive for its food, but filter-fed in shallow lakes and waterways. It is also thought to have been a strong flyer.

Moko *Porphyrio mantelli* (illustrated in Chapter 11)

The South Island species of takahe was once thought to be extinct as it had not been seen for 50 years, and was only known from four Fiordland sightings; it was later rediscovered in 1948. The North Island species of takahe, named moko by Maori, has never been seen by Europeans, and is known only from midden sites, a two-million-year-old fossil found on the east coast, and a possible sighting in 1894. Hunted into extinction, it was flightless, like its South Island cousin, but was taller and more slender in build. A second flock of Australian swamp hens, from which it originally descended, arrived in New Zealand about the time that Maori arrived, and these are commonly known as pukeko (not illustrated).

New Zealand coot *Fulica prisca* (not illustrated)

As coots go, the New Zealand coot was a very large coot indeed. It is known from fossil finds in the North and South islands, as well as the Chathams, to which it must have flown from the mainland. (Later, like the mainland birds, it attained a much larger size, and lost the power of flight.)

The most notable characteristic of coots the world over is the white frontal shield between the eyes. Coots also have lobes along each toe, which help them swim, rather than webbed feet like ducks. Lobed toes are a feature shared by the grebes, which are not related. Like grebes, however, coots are good swimmers and they have a delightful habit of nodding their heads as they progress through the water. Their preferred habitats are wetlands with enclosed water generously fringed with reed cover, where they nest on floating platforms of vegetation. The New Zealand flightless coot was hastened to extinction by early Maori who took them for food; once again, the evidence has been found in middens.

Hodgen's waterhen *Gallinula hodgenorum* (not illustrated)

Maori middens have also been the source of several finds of this now-extinct bird, in both the North and South islands. It was named for Messrs Hodgen, who were the owners of the property on which the first find was recorded. This rail was a flightless moorhen, almost certainly descended from a flock of Australian black-tailed native hens that flew across the Tasman Sea thousands of years ago, and, like so many other native New Zealand birds, evolved to become flightless after their arrival. When rails are startled, they never fly to safety, but scurry secretively into nearby undergrowth. As it adapted to its adoptive habitat in New Zealand, Hodgen's waterhen would have settled well into the wetlands, which, unlike Australian wetlands, almost never suffer from a seasonal shortage of water.

Chapter 14

MOUNT TARAWERA ERUPTS

10 June 1886

STRADDLING THE BOUNDARY BETWEEN the Australian and the Pacific plates, New Zealand is the emergent part of the sunken continent of Zealandia. The Australian Plate is slowly moving in a northerly direction, while the Pacific Plate is bearing west. This means that both plates are moving towards, and past, each other; the result is major tectonic collision.

South of Milford Sound the Pacific Plate is overriding the Australian Plate. In a straight line down the west coast of the South Island, along the Alpine Fault, the two plates are slipping past one another. To date, this action has slowly pushed up the continental crust at least 20,000 metres, in an uplift that has been occurring for three to five million years.

North of North Canterbury, the Australian Plate is overriding the Pacific Plate, forcing it deep beneath the Earth's crust where the temperatures are hot enough to melt crustal rocks. The result is that from the central North Island, and continuing beneath the sea as far north as the Equator, volcanoes have formed, marking a line parallel to the plate boundary which here runs slightly off the south-eastern shore of the southern North Island. From time to time, they still erupt. Indeed, all around the margin of the Pacific Ocean, the 'Ring of Fire' marked by the plate boundary has produced volcanoes – in Alaska, Japan, Indonesia, the Philippines, Peru, Chile and Antarctica. The Kermadec Islands far to the north, and White Island, an active volcano lying a mere 40 kilometres offshore, mark the northernmost part of the active line in New Zealand territory, and from there it continues in an almost straight line as far south as the Tongariro National Park, the heart of the volcanic plateau.

Within the zone lies the giant volcano of Taupo, sleeping beneath its caldera lake, beyond the southern shores of which rise three prominent cones, Tongariro, Ngauruhoe and Ruapehu, any one of which is liable to erupt at any time.

New Zealand's volcanic heart

The Earth's crust in the Rotorua–Taupo area is probably only 5–10 kilometres thick, and magma chambers are relatively close to the surface. Groundwater lying within the granular and fractured crustal volcanic rocks becomes heated and rises to the surface where it is discharged from many boiling water basins and geysers, hot springs and mud pools. Such thermal water contains large amounts

Opposite: The White Terrace was a stairway of semicircular silica terraces that descended from a large geyser cauldron. Each glistening white step enclosed a basin of shimmering turquoise water, which emerged from the geyser at boiling point and grew gradually cooler as it cascaded down to Lake Rotomahana, nestled at the foot of Mt Tarawera. On the western side of the lake rose the slightly smaller Pink Terrace, whose large upper basins were utilised by bathers. While waiting for the canoe to ferry them back to their hotel, five tourists are being guided by Kate Middlemass, a part-Maori guide. This illustration is based on black-and-white photographs taken prior to the 1886 eruption, and on the superb paintings of Charles Blomfield.

of dissolved silica, and upon reaching the surface this distinctive substance is often deposited to form rock – known as sinter – in beautiful formations. Nowhere else in the world than at Lake Rotomahana, less than 20 kilometres from the township of Rotorua, however, were there formed silica sinter terraces as beautiful as the famous Pink and White Terraces.

'The tattooed rock' . . .

Lake Rotomahana was an irregular shape scarcely 2 kilometres long, and its waters were warm as a result of two startlingly beautiful sinter terraces: one coloured white, the other in delicate shades of pink. Both terraces were washed daily with the water discharged by large hot springs at their summits.

The White Terraces comprised the larger of the two formations. They lay among the fern and tea-trees that grew on the lake's north-eastern shore where most of the thermal activity was found, and formed a glistening white staircase that covered nearly 3.5 hectares. The Maori who lived in the vicinity called them Te Tarata, 'the tattooed rock'. At the top of the staircase lay a large cauldron where an impressive geyser frequently erupted, hurling out boiling water and steam, the latter rising high into the sky.

A geyser eruption was heralded by deep rumbling and gurgling that grew steadily louder until at last, in a fountain of boiling water, the geyser burst into life. The boiling water soon filled the cauldron until it overflowed down the glistening stairway of semicircular silica terraces. Each terrace formed a shallow basin enclosed with a raised lip, and as it filled to the brim, the water cascaded on down, eventually spilling into the lake below. As if these exquisite shimmering white creations sculpted by nature weren't perfect enough, the water they contained was of a delightful turquoise shade.

. . . and the 'cloud in the heavens'

The Pink Terraces covered more than 2 hectares and bore the poetic Maori name Otukapuarangi, which means 'cloud in the heavens'. The lower terraces lacked basins, and were more like shallow stairs leading down the hillside to end at the lake's edge. Remarkably, these terraces were coloured in shades of pink and were thought to be the more beautiful. At the top of this staircase, the terraces were almost white, and the colours intensified as one descended towards the lake below. The silica-rich water that flowed over these terraces was softer and 'silkier' than the water that had helped create the White Terraces. Near the top were several bath-like basins, that came to be used for exactly that purpose by nineteenth-century tourists, who would undress to immerse themselves in the soft water. Victorian decorum was strictly observed: while women bathed, the men inspected other thermal springs near the foot of the silica cascade. Afterwards they exchanged roles.

Early Maori settlers found the Rotorua–Taupo area most suitable places to live. The fumaroles and boiling water basins were ideal places for cooking the flesh of the many birds that lived in the forests, and the fish and eels they found in the streams and lakes. Bathing in the warm-water pools was a popular activity. Several villages once dotted the shores of Lake Rotomahana, and their houses had been sited in locations were the ground was warm – an especial boon during winter. Also, like the Europeans who arrived later, the early Maori found that bathing in the thermal waters eased skin ailments and the aches of rheumatism and arthritis.

The Eighth Wonder of the World

Such was the popularity of the terraces among European tourists and settlers that they became known as the 'Eighth Wonder of the World', attracting increasing numbers of visitors during the nineteenth century. Among the most notable of these were Governor Sir George Grey and Prince Alfred, second son

Below: The eruption of Mt Tarawera as it would have appeared at about 2.10 am on the night of 10 June 1886. The viewpoint for this illustration, based on a photograph by Josiah Martin, is above the western shore of Lake Tarawera, and based on eyewitness descriptions and photographs of volcanic lightning. This painting first appeared on the cover of the book Tarawera, *written and published by Professor R. F. Keam.*

of Queen Victoria, the latter accompanied by then Governor Sir George Bowen (whose wife, Lady Bowen, inspired the naming of the Bowen Falls in Milford Sound). Another important visitor was the Austrian geologist Ferdinand von Hochstetter who was the only scientist to map and describe the Rotomahana springs in detail.

Photographers brought bulky cameras to take sharp black-and-white photographs on glass negatives, and recorded their visits with prints that have become national treasures. (One famous visitor was the American author Mark Twain, who is said to have had himself photographed bathing naked, superimposed alongside two Maori maidens – also bathing. He sent the doctored photograph to a friend, inscribed with the words, 'This is how I take my bath every day in New Zealand.')

During the Christmas period of 1884, Charles Blomfield, one of New Zealand's finest landscape artists, visited the terraces with his daughter Mary. Blomfield finished a number of paintings of the two terraces, and made numerous

Above: The steaming cliffs of Lake Rotomahana. When Tarawera erupted, this lake, which lay alongside the volcano, was considerably altered in the upheaval, and is now believed to be at least twice as deep. Almost directly above where the Pink Terraces once lay, thermal activity has produced sinter formations which may just signal the beginning of new terrace formations.

sketches. After they were destroyed by the eruption of Mount Tarawera in 1886, Blomfield completed several more paintings after referring to his earlier paintings and sketches, and it is he whom we must thank for the only extensive full-colour portrayal of these two masterpieces of nature.

The Rotomahana basin was drained northwards by a river known as the Kaiwaka Stream, whose banks were fringed with native trees and shrubs. The stream's sources were Rotomakariri, ('Cold Lake'), and Rotomahana ('Warm Lake'), in whose silica-rich and warm waters no fish were able to survive.

The Phantom Canoe

Lakes Tarawera and Rotomahana lie in the shadow of the forbidding and almost bare bulk of Mount Tarawera. Until the night of 10 June 1886, neither Maori nor European settlers realised that Tarawera was in fact a sleeping volcano. Indeed, when high-ranking villagers died, they were generally buried in recesses high up on Mount Tarawera. But the entire area around Lake Rotomahana and Mount Tarawera is geologically unstable. Outbursts of thermal activity and earthquakes had always been relatively common there. These events were given supernatural significance by the Maori that lived in the area.

One strange happening that has been given many explanations was the appearance of the so-called 'Phantom Canoe' on the lake. This took place on 31 May 1886, several days before the eruption.

To reach the Pink and White Terraces from the usual starting place of Te Wairoa near the western shores of Lake Tarawera, tourists paid to be paddled in a Maori-crewed whale boat across the lake to a strip of land, where they landed and walked to their destination. On the day in question, tourists guided by the famous Maori guide Sophia were out on Lake Tarawera when gradually a large waka (Maori canoe) appeared, apparently filled with Maori paddlers.

The passengers in the tourist party included an Auckland priest, six Maori paddlers, three Maori women and several tourists. The Europeans thought this apparition was a war canoe, but the Maori travellers thought it was a 'spirit canoe'. The accounts given by all who saw the 'phantom' became more fanciful as the years went by, and moreover conflicted: some said there was mist on the water, others disagreed. Perhaps the only point on which all witnesses agreed was that it was a large waka, paddled by Maori, and that for some time its path across the lake was nearly parallel to their own, and that although Maori members in their own boat hailed it, they received no reply. The 'phantom' then passed behind a headland and was lost from view.

The mountain ripped open

Several days later at one o'clock in the morning on 10 June, people in the vicinity of Mount Tarawera were awoken by a series of earthquakes. The Te Wairoa schoolmaster Charles Haszard, his wife, their five children and a young nephew lived in the substantial schoolhouse, which had been built on a small hill overlooking Lake Tarawera. They, too, were rudely awoken by the earthquakes. They quickly dressed and moved out onto the verandah overlooking the lake where on its far shore rose Mount Tarawera. At first they saw an enormous black cloud form over the mountain, lit by numerous flashes of lightning and speeding fireballs. Before their eyes, the mountain was being ripped open by what finally became a 17-kilometre-long rift, and from it were thrown huge amounts of volcanic mud, ash and red-hot rocks that fell all around, peppering the surrounding landscape.

The hotels and private dwellings at Te Wairoa were destroyed by the heavy showers of scoria stones, which lasted for about an hour (according to an eyewitness account), and then buried under the mud. Similarly, in the Maori settlements surrounding Lake Tarawera all but one of their inhabitants were buried alive or killed by falling rocks. Suddenly a huge rift opened up beneath Lake Rotomahana and the subsequent volcanic explosions quickly destroyed the famous Pink and White Terraces.

The precise death toll on that night will never be known, but it is estimated that about 120 Maori and Pakeha lost their lives. Among the latter were Charles Haszard and three of his children, as well as Edwin Bainbridge, a young English tourist, who was crushed by the verandah of McRae's Hotel in Te Wairoa, which collapsed on him.

The eruption of Mount Tarawera dealt a severe blow to the fledgling New Zealand tourist trade. Nevertheless, new shrubs and trees have emerged through the volcanic mud, and although no more than 120 or so years old, this native forest is becoming more attractive as the years go by. The lake of Rotomahana is now many times its former size. The valley of Waimangu, named for the world's tallest geyser, which played for several years following the eruption, is a wonderful tourist attraction in its own right, with boiling lakes, geysers and vents – as well as what are the beginnings of tiny new sinter terraces.

Chapter 15

Recently Lost Birds and Rarities

1840 to today

New Zealand's forests must once have rung with the most beautiful and melodious birdsong imaginable. After the last ice age ended some 10,000 years ago, the land became an avian paradise. There were no known mammalian predators – and certainly no snakes – to prey on ground-nesting adults and nestlings or steal eggs. And as the temperatures rose and the cold released its grip on the land, a range of new habitats for birds, including wetlands, lowland forests and alpine forests, was able to flourish.

Land of birds

As an inevitable result of the tectonic upheavals that were continuing to shape the land, populations of birds became geographically isolated from one another, leading to speciation. Several bird groups speciated on either side of Cook Strait, the stretch of sea that separates the North and South islands. One example is the yellowhead (*Mohoua ocrocephala*) and whitehead (*Mohoua albicilla*). The two species share a common ancestor, whose population, over a period of time, became broken up. Individuals in the South Island acquired bright yellow plumage on the head, breast and tail: they became yellowheads. Individuals restricted to the North Island's forests developed into whiteheads – with a white head and greyish-white breast. Sadly, the yellowhead is becoming extremely rare in mainland forests, and soon may be found only in offshore island sanctuaries such as Stewart Island's Ulva Island.

The kokako is another bird that acquired different livery in each of the two main islands. The northern bird has blue wattles, whereas its southern counterpart developed orange wattles. The South Island bird has not been sighted for many years and is now believed to be extinct.

With the exception of alpine areas, forests covered the land from the mountain foothills down to the coastline. These forests would have been home to millions of birds. Considering the size of the New Zealand land mass, there were relatively few species, but their populations were very high, due to the lack of mammalian predators or competitors and to the benign environment. Almost the world over, the end of the 167-million-year reign of the dinosaurs heralded the rise and rise of mammals; but not so in New Zealand, where the ecological niches normally occupied by mammals were exploited instead by birds.

Opposite: New Zealand's most recently lost birds, clockwise from top right: huia pair (male with the shorter bill), last seen in 1907; South Island kokako, declared extinct in 2007; Stephens Island wren (left), last seen in 1900; bush wren (right, 1964); New Zealand quail (1860); Stewart Island snipe (1960); New Zealand snipe (1870); New Zealand little bittern (1890); South Island piopio (left, 1905); North Island piopio (right, 1902); whekau or laughing owl (1950s).

Killer kiore and kuri

When Maori settlers arrived, they brought the kiore or Polynesian rat (*Rattus exulans*), whose taste for bird flesh meant that several smaller bird species were preyed upon, with disastrous results. For centuries Polynesian people had lived on islands that likewise had no mammalian predators, and they would have been adept at snaring birds for food, just as they were at catching fish. One can only imagine their delight upon arrival in this land to discover forests that were alive with birds – especially inquisitive flightless species that had never seen humans and were slow to flee. And so the carnage began. The Maori required food, and were largely unaware that their actions would put paid to the unique bird life. In a little less than 600 years, more than half of the native bird species had either become extinct or were on the verge of extinction.

Admittedly, Maori eventually practised a form of bird conservation – they did not take some species in the breeding season – but in the main their efforts came too late. Mammals that Maori brought with them in their canoes became predators themselves. The kiore raided the nests of many species of ground-nesting birds, and the dog they called kuri hunted the kiwi, kakapo and other smallish flightless species.

Predators from Europe

When European settlers began to arrive in 1840, they brought with them two further rat species, the large Norway rat (*Rattus norvegicus*) and the roof or ship rat (*Rattus rattus*). Other intruders included cats – notorious bird killers – and more dogs, which attacked all flightless bird species. European settlers also brought rabbits for gentlemen farmers to hunt in their spare time. Rabbit numbers, unchecked by predators, exploded, especially on the upland farms of Otago and Canterbury. As a consequence, the government of the day quickly approved the release of stoats to control them – but this 'solution', seemingly a good idea at the time, would have disastrous consequences. The cunning stoats soon found it quicker to pounce on native birds foraging unsuspectingly on the forest floor than to spend hours searching for rab-

Below: The kakapo is flightless, nocturnal and the world's largest parrot. When humans arrived in New Zealand 750 years ago, it would have been one of the most common birds of the night. By the early 1980s, however, kakapo numbers had dropped to barely more than 50 birds. Fortunately, through the efforts of Don Merton and the Department of Conservation's recovery programme, numbers have increased to more than 80 individuals.

bits down long twisting burrows. Springtime, a season when many female birds nested on or close to the open forest floor, was a time of great feasting for female stoats gathering meat for their young. Stoats were also adept at climbing trees, putting further species at risk.

Native pigeons, destined for the pot, fell to the settlers' guns. Vast tracts of native forest either fell to the axe, or were deliberately set on fire in order to 'clear the land'. However, a forest contains more than trees, and untold numbers of birds perished in the flames. The often-quoted farmers' credo, 'If it moves, shoot it; if it's growing, cut it down!' was never truer.

From 1840 onwards, large numbers of domestic fowl were imported so that settlers would have a plentiful supply of eggs and poultry. These domestic fowls are thought to have introduced avian diseases, which soon found their way into populations of native birds, which had no resistance to the unfamiliar viruses.

By the 1880s it was noticed that populations of several bird species were fast disappearing. By that decade's end, the North Island saddleback, once common in native forests, was to be found only on Mana Island (also known by its European name Hen Island, the largest of the Hen and Chickens group in the Hauraki Gulf). Similarly, the stitchbird or hihi, once common in North Island forests, was soon to be found only on Little Barrier Island. (This island has the poetic Maori name Hauturu, 'resting place of the wind'. It became New Zealand's first and most important wildlife sanctuary when ownership passed to the Crown in 1894.) Both species have since made remarkable recoveries thanks to the careful preservation of predator-free island sanctuaries, established through the efforts of the Department of Conservation. Many other species were not so fortunate, and it has been estimated that more than 40 per cent of endemic New Zealand birds have become extinct – primarily at the hands of humans, the domestic cat and the kiore – since settlement began. Here follows a selection of forest bird extinctions that have occurred after 1840.

New Zealand little bittern (*Ixobrychus novaezelandiae*)

New Zealand has one largish species of bittern, measuring 710 millimetres from bill tip to tail tip. It is called the Australasian bittern, because the same species occurs in both countries. Bitterns are strictly wetland birds and their food consists of small freshwater fish and animals that they catch in shallow waters. They are more often heard than seen, uttering loud booming noises but remaining hidden by virtue of their camouflaging plumage, which closely matches the surroundings in which they live. In the past, New Zealand was also home to the little bittern, which had quite different plumage from the little bittern that occurs in Australia. The New Zealand bird was small, and was approximately 300 millimetres in length. In European times, almost all sightings of this small bittern occurred in South Island's Westland, where no more than 20 were collected. Subfossil bones have been collected only from the North Island.

Above: The New Zealand little bittern. The causes of its extinction, which took place before 1900, are not clear.

New Zealand quail (*Coturnix novaezelandiae*)

In 1840, settlers reported that the New Zealand quail was 'excessively' abundant in parts of both the main islands. It gradually disappeared from the landscape during the 1870s, and within a few years this beautiful little quail was deemed to be extinct. Certainly, it was 'excessively' hunted, but as it had a high reproductive rate, the disappearance is hard to fathom. Possible culprits include exotic gamebirds that brought in avian diseases, and possibly also rats. (Like most quails, this bird spent almost all of its life on the ground, where it also nested.) Some ornithologists have suggested that the New Zealand quail was the same species as the Australian stubble quail (*Coturnix pectoralis*). However, a careful study of the illustration by the nineteenth-century artist J. G. Keulemans clearly shows that the plumage of the two differs in almost every respect.

Laughing owl (*Sceloglaux albifacies*)

The laughing owl, known to Maori as whekau, was very aptly named by settlers, given the distinctive chuckling sounds it made during the night. It is also reported to have made doleful shrieks, barked like a dog and mewed like a cat. Prior to the arrival of humans, this bird occurred throughout the three main New Zealand islands and probably offshore islands too. (A peak on Little Barrier Island in the Hauraki Gulf bears the name Whekauwhekau.) Following European settlement, the laughing owl was sighted only in areas east of the Southern Alps and twice in the southern part of the North Island, but may have lived on into the 1950s.

Above: The laughing owl was about twice the size of the only other native New Zealand owl, the ruru or morepork. Apparently it was not difficult to keep in captivity, being gentle and easily handled.

Huia (*Heteralocha acutirostris*)

The huia has quite a claim to fame. It was the only known bird in the world in which the two sexes had such markedly different bills. Whereas the female's bill was long and down-curved, that of the male bird was a little less than half the size, yet was stronger. The extra strength allowed the male to chisel a hole in the trunk of a tree, enabling the female to insert her long and more slender bill in order to take hold of a grub, which she then pulled out in order to feed her mate. Huia were found only in the North Island, where they were once quite common. Maori hunted them for food, and also prized their tail feathers, which were regarded as sacred and therefore worn only by individuals of high standing. European milliners paid collectors handsomely for dead huia, after a fashion sprang up for wearing the tail feathers in hats, following a visit in 1896 by Prince Albert, who after receiving a gift of huia feathers placed them in his hatband. This handsome bird was a poor flyer, unafraid of humans, and it readily came down from the trees when called: frailties that effectively doomed it. The last sighting of a live huia was made in December 1907.

Piopio (*Turnagra capensis, T. turnagra*)

There were once two species of piopio: the South Island (*T. capensis*) and the North Island (*T. turnagra*). The former had the more colourful plumage, whereas the latter was reportedly the better songster – indeed, it was said to be New Zealand's finest songbird. (It must have been remarkably good to have excelled the songs of the kokako, bellbird and tui!) For many years New Zealand ornithologists thought the genus might have been a member of the thrush family because of a superficial resemblance. After careful study by American experts, however, they placed it in the bower bird/bird-of-paradise family, of which it was the most primitive member. With grim predictability, populations of this marvellous songster plummeted after the arrival of European settlers (or, more precisely, the ship rats and mustelids that accompanied them), and the last confirmed sighting was made in the early 1900s.

New Zealand wrens (*Xenicus* species)

This entry refers to the extinction of yet five more native bird species, the first two of which feature in the illustration: Lyall's wren and the bush wren. New Zealand wrens were misnamed in that the birds in this family of endemic birds belonging in the genus *Xenicus* are not wrens at all, but an extremely primitive family of birds known only from New Zealand. A further two species, the long-billed wren and stout-legged wren, both died out after the arrival of Maori.

The extinction of the Stephens Island wren, the only wholly flightless perching bird known, came about when in 1900 the keeper for the newly built lighthouse took up his post on the island, accompanied by his cat; a few months later, the world's entire population of Stephens Island wrens was extinct. The bush wren was once found throughout New Zealand, although the North Island species had become rare by the time of European settlement. The South Island bird was widespread when European settlers arrived, but declined rapidly in number thereafter, and by 1967 was confined to Big South Cape, a small island close to Stewart Island. The bird was common there until rats arrived on fishing vessels, and the bird was declared extinct in 1968. This leaves the highly endangered rock wren (*Xenicus gilviventris*) and the rifleman (*Acanthisitta chloris*), the only surviving members of this unique New Zealand family.

Many of the birds mentioned above can be found in *Buller's Birds*, a volume written by the nineteenth-century ornithologist Walter Buller. Many people have assumed that Buller himself provided the exquisite illustrations for his book, but these were in fact the work of artist/lithographer J. G. Keulemans. The 2006 publication of *The Art of J. G. Keulemans*, with an introduction by Ross Galbreath, has helped to set the record straight, and although it has taken more than 100 years, New Zealanders are now gaining the greatest respect for this remarkable artist.

Above: Black robin (Petroica traversi). *Once widespread throughout the Chatham Islands, by the 1870s numbers of black robin had shrunk considerably, and the birds were found only on Mangere and Little Mangere islands. By 1976, there were only five birds left alive with only one breeding pair – a female named 'Old Blue' and a male named 'Old Yellow'. Fortunately, the innovative techniques of the Department of Conservation's wildlife officer Don Merton and his team of assistants saved this bird from extinction. Through his efforts and the help of tomtits who became the robin's foster parents, the black robin population today now numbers more than 250 individuals.*

Chapter 16

THE HAWKE'S BAY EARTHQUAKE

3 February 1931

SINCE 1843 THE ENTIRE NEW ZEALAND region has experienced more than 160 earthquakes of magnitude 6.5 or more on the Richter scale. That figure equates on average to one major quake every year or so. At least 12 of these have been in or near Hawke's Bay. On 3 February 1931, Hawke's Bay was struck by the most devastating earthquake in New Zealand's recorded history. The magnitude 6.8 earthquake shook the area in two tremors at least 30 seconds apart, and a further 674 aftershocks shook the area within the next two months. In all, the quakes killed an estimated 256 people. An exploration into the region's geological and human history helps explain the circumstances that led to the tragedy.

To the west of Hawke's Bay lies a range of mountains, and lying between the mountains and the sea are the Heretaunga Plains. Prior to 1931, large stretches of swampland lay at the eastern edge of the plains, fed by rivers that ran eastward from the mountains to the sea, and originally carried rocks and boulders that were worn smooth as they travelled. Eventually, they were piled by the sea to form two spits that reached an island lying several kilometres offshore. Maori had lived in the area for several hundred years, as fish were plentiful in the lagoon and the bay which lay beyond; their diet was supplemented by the large number of eels which were plentiful in the rivers and swamps. When early European settlers arrived in the 1840s, the two rocky spits formed the coastline between the lagoon and the open sea.

Rise of the twin cities

During the late nineteenth century, the government of the day had been busy purchasing Maori-owned land in order to establish towns. The land on which Napier came to be built was made up of three distinct areas. The first was a triangular piece of land that lay between the swamp and an island, which in fact was a small hill rising from the sea, connected to the land by the aforementioned rocky spits. The second was another triangle of land north of the island on which were scattered many small lagoons; the third was the hill itself.

A mere 20 kilometres to the south of Napier, and some distance from the coast, the city of Hastings sprang up, founded on the rich land of the Heretaunga Plains. Over the years, Napier and Hastings kept pace with one another, spreading out in area as their populations rose. Napier now has a fine port and

Opposite: This illustration is based on a black-and-white photograph taken by Napier resident Norman Every approximately 45 minutes after the Hawke's Bay earthquake struck on the morning of 3 February 1931. The car in the foreground was a 1924 Buick Coupe, and the owner left his vehicle immediately in order to assist in rescue work. When he eventually returned to his car, it was engulfed in flames, along with entire blocks of Napier's commercial district. The fireman in the original photograph is believed to be Superintendent Gilberd, being chased by flames along Hastings Street.

is the administrative base for the two cities, while Hastings has become the service centre for the many market gardens, orchards and farms that have become established on the fertile plains.

By the 1920s Napier's population had swelled to more than 16,000, and the city boasted many imposing buildings such as the Courthouse and St Patrick's Roman Catholic Church; both were built from timber, like many of the houses. Napier's other fine buildings were St John's Anglican Cathedral built in 1888 and the two Municipal Theatres (1912), one of which boasted more than 1,000 seats. Also of note were the Boys' High School and hostel (1926) and St Paul's Presbyterian Church, which opened its doors in 1931. Although architects had ensured that many of these buildings had some reinforcing incorporated into their designs, most of the minor buildings in the centre were constructed with non-reinforced bricks and concrete. Façades were decorated with heavy masonry ornaments and cornices, which overhung the footpaths below.

Such was the profile of the two cities before 3 February 1931. As for the land beneath them, it has a geological history of great upheavals: just a few million years ago, the entire area encompassing Hawke's Bay lay beneath the sea, and was raised above the surface by degrees over many years, in a series of jolts and shudders, as a product of tectonic processes. In short, it is one of the most seismically active areas in the country.

Sitting as it does upon the boundary of two tectonic plates, the whole of New Zealand lies within a 200-kilometre-wide seismological zone. In the North Island, the boundary between the subducting Pacific Plate and the overriding Australian Plate is located a mere 150 kilometres to the east of Napier, beneath the sea. This zone is known as the Hikurangi Trough, and its close proximity to the Hawke's Bay region is the reason why the whole area is subject to so many large earth tremors.

The two plates are constantly moving against each other at 20–50 millimetres each year, and although this movement is slow, nevertheless it is constant, causing immense strains to build up at the boundary. The strains are relieved only when something 'gives', in the form of an earthquake: a sudden and violent fracture, or slippage. The surface on which the slippage occurs is known as a fault: a plane of shattered and sheared rock. In Hawke's Bay, the landward side of the boundary is riddled with many faults, each of which may be up to 100 metres wide. They lie roughly parallel to one another, forming a great fault system that is connected at depth within the Earth.

Shaky region

English settlers first arrived in Wellington in 1840, and gradually spread north and east to take up farming lots in Hawke's Bay. It would not be long before they experienced the effects of the active fault systems. On 8 July 1843, a large earthquake struck western Hawke's Bay, causing cracks in the ground at

Napier and landslides on the cliffs at Cape Kidnappers. A second large earthquake struck Wellington and the Wairarapa region in 1855 when a magnitude 8.2 earthquake, centred 30 kilometres south-east of Wellington, sent shock waves that were felt as far as Hawke's Bay. This was the largest historic earthquake recorded in New Zealand. Eight years later on 23 February 1863, a magnitude 7.5 quake struck Hawke's Bay. This rattled Napier, toppling chimneys from their foundations, and causing landslides and surface faulting in the area.

On 4 August 1904, a magnitude 7.2 earthquake was centred inland from nearby Cape Turnagain. Once more, Napier, just over 100 kilometres to the north, lost several chimneys, and the nearby town of Mohaka was hit by a small tsunami that may have been generated by a landslide at Cape Kidnappers.

The 1931 quake

February is usually the hottest month of New Zealand's summer, and 1931 was no exception for the population of Hawke's Bay, who were also in the grip of a prolonged drought. As so often is recorded before a major earthquake strikes, the morning of Tuesday 3 February was hot and still. No birds were singing in the trees, animals became restless, and locals noticed that the ocean was unusually calm after several days of unexplained turbulence.

The earthquake struck at 10.47 in the morning, and almost immediately the neat rows of stone buildings were reduced to piles of shattered concrete, broken bricks and piles of rubble. Clouds of smoke and choking dust rose into the air. Many of the downtown office workers who ran into the streets were instantly killed by falling masonry as stone decorations tumbled from buildings.

A handsome nurses' home, completed only a year before, was an important new health facility in Napier. Designed in the Spanish Mission style, the building had been hailed as an architectural masterpiece, but it was found later to have been riddled with design faults, lacking the reinforcements to withstand even a moderate earthquake. On the morning of the earthquake, 16 nurses were asleep inside, having worked the night shift at the nearby hospital. As the earthquake struck, the building collapsed into a heap of rubble, killing eight nurses, along with three office workers downstairs.

For schoolchildren, it had been the first day of the new term; luckily, however, the earthquake struck just as most children were outside their classrooms enjoying a mid-morning break. The exception was the three-storied Napier Technical School. Although many students had escaped when the building finally collapsed like a pack of cards, nine were killed and many more were injured.

Hastings was also violently rocked. The *New Zealand Herald* reported that the city 'was full of shoppers when the disaster occurred, and they were caught like rats in a trap'. The main shopping street was all but destroyed, and the cries of trapped women and children could be heard among the ruins.

Napier's port came in for damage, too. Before the disaster, it was divided

Above: Norfolk Island pine. This splendid tree, native to Norfolk Island, was introduced into New Zealand early in European settlement. It was planted as a street tree in Napier during the 1890s especially to line the newly built Marine Parade. This specimen survived the 1931 earthquake.

between two harbours. To the west of the city lay the Ahuriri Lagoon, 3,000 hectares of mudflats that was a favoured area for picnicking, as well as boating on the full tide. The inner harbour was open to large ships, which would moor at the wharf before discharging or loading cargo; the outer harbour was able to berth substantial vessels. On the morning of 3 February, HMS *Veronica* had entered the inner harbour and berthed. Immediately, there came a sound as of a loud explosion, and the crew rushed up onto the decks to be confronted by what some thought must be the end of the world. The wharf buckled, twisted and then partially collapsed. Buildings and houses began to buckle, and then they, too, fell into heaps of rubble. The walls of the fully laden wool stores built on the wharf contorted and burst, spilling wool bales onto the heaving dockside and into the sea – which, incredibly, was fast disappearing.

One of the strangest episodes occurred in the harbour where the *Northumberland* was at anchor after spending several days loading a cargo of frozen meat. As the earthquake progressed, the lagoon emptied, and the entire area began to be uplifted by some 1.5 metres. It was then that the sailors lining the decks saw the wreck of a ship suddenly emerge from the mud. By an extraordinary coincidence, it was another *Northumberland*; the sailors easily read the name on the stern of the wreck. Then, just as suddenly, the sea bottom opened up and, with a loud slurping noise, swallowed the entire hulk once more. It was later ascertained that the *Northumberland* hulk had been a fully rigged iron freighter before it was wrecked off the coast of Napier 44 years earlier.

As the sea receded, the Ahuriri Lagoon was soon drained, exposing about 1,300 hectares of the sea floor. (Since the earthquake, a further 1,700 hectares has been reclaimed.) The now exposed seabed presented an extraordinary sight. Thousands of horse mussels, half buried in the mud, were surrounded by not only millions of shellfish, but also thousands of every type of lagoon fish, stranded and flapping. Within a couple of days the hot, still air was filled with the overpowering stench of rotting fish.

The centre of Napier presented an appalling sight. Collapsed buildings lay in mounds of broken bricks, smashed concrete beams, piles of shattered lengths of timber, and crushed vehicles. Dust choked the air, and fires broke out in some of the wrecked downtown pharmacies, the result of overturned Bunsen burners. (At that time, during shop hours, chemists kept Bunsen burners constantly alight for use in the preparation of medicines. Although electricity immediately ceased in overhead power lines, and gas pipes were ruptured, there was enough gas to keep overturned Bunsen burners alight for some time.)

Today, Napier is arguably one of the world's finest cities built in the Art Deco style, which had become fashionable during the 1930s and remains a drawcard for visitors to the city today. The clean and uncluttered style has proved not only to be enduring but also ideally suited to the rebuilding of a city that is prone to earthquakes.

GLOSSARY

ammonite – extinct **cephalopod mollusc**, with a flat spiral shell.

amphibian – **vertebrate** animal belonging to the class Amphibia, usually having an aquatic larval stage. Amphibians were the first vertebrates to leave the sea and walk on land; today they include frogs, toads, salamanders, etc.

angiosperm – flowering plant.

archipelago – group of islands.

asteroid – minor planet in orbit around the Sun.

atmosphere – layer of gases surrounding a planet.

baleen – coarse hair-like fronds sprouting from gums of certain whales, creating a sieve-like structure that is used in straining small prey items from seawater.

basalt – common igneous rock, commonly produced from volcanic eruption (as in Auckland region).

belemnite – extinct **cephalopod mollusc** with streamlined squid-like form.

bivalve – a water-dwelling **mollusc** encased within two flattened shells joined by a hinge.

calcareous – containing calcium carbonate.

caldera – a volcanic collapse structure formed by the rapid eruption of a **magma chamber**.

cephalopod – **mollusc** with a head surrounded by tentacles, i.e. squid, octopus, nautilus, **ammonite**, etc.

cetacean – member of the marine mammal order Cetacea: the whales and dolphins.

chelonian – reptile of the order Chelonia, including turtles (marine), tortoises (terrestrial) and terrapins (freshwater).

crustacean – animal belonging to the class Crustacea, usually with a hard shell; examples include crabs, lobsters and slaters.

cycad – palm-like plant of ancient origin.

echinoderm – marine **invertebrate** with symmetrical body plan; includes sea stars, sea urchins (kina), etc.

echolocation – techique in which an animal (i.e. dolphin or bat) emits sounds and then analyses their echoes to form a mental 'map' of the surroundings.

elasmobranch – member of a group of cartilaginous fishes, which include the sharks, rays, skates and chimeras.

eon – major unit of geological time, containing **eras**.

epiphyte – plant that lives supported on another plant (such as a tree), rather than rooted in soil.

epoch – unit of geological time, subdivision of a **period**.

era – unit of geological time, containing **periods**; a subdivision of an **eon**.

fault – fracture line in bedrock created by **tectonic** stresses in Earth's crust.

fauna – assembly of different animal **species**.

flora – assembly of different plant **species**.

gastrolith – stone swallowed and kept in an animal's gut or stomach, where its grinding action against other stones helps grind food into a digestible form.

genus – group containing one or more animal or plant **species**.

gymnosperm – plant of ancient origin, with seed unprotected by an ovary. (The name means 'naked seed'.) Includes conifers, cycads, ginkgo, etc.

hot spot – site on Earth's surface where plume of rising **magma** creates localised volcanic activity.

ice age – periodic cooling of Earth's climate accompanied by freezing temperatures.

igneous – (of or relating to) rock created by volcanic activity; basalt is the most common of the igneous rocks.

interglacial – period of time between one ice age and the next.

invertebrate – animal lacking a vertebra (backbone).

lava – ejected, solidified **magma**.

lycopod, lycopodium – clubmoss, a flowerless plant of ancient origin.

magma – molten rock under ground (which, when ejected from volcano and cooled, becomes lava).

magma chamber – underground mass of molten rock.

mekosuchine – (of or relating to) an extinct group of crocodiles living in south-west Pacific until around 2,000 years ago

metamorphic – (of or relating to) rock that has undergone change after being subjected to heat or pressure.

mollusc – **invertebrate** with a soft body and usually a hard outer shell. Slugs, snails and **cephalopods** (octopus, squid, nautilus) are all molluscs.

odontocete – member of the toothed whales (i.e. dolphins, orca, sperm whale, etc.).

pa – Maori hilltop fortress.

period – unit of geological time, containing **epochs**; a subdivision of an **era**.

photosynthesis – process by which plants, using energy from the Sun, convert carbon dioxide and water into carbohydrates.

phreatomagmatic eruption – explosive eruption in which **magma** comes into contact with superheated underground water.

phytoplankton – collective name for various plants or plant-like life forms that populate ocean waters and generally live by **photosynthesis**.

plankton – *see* **phytoplankton**, **zooplankton**.

podocarp – any of several coniferous trees whose fruits (cones) sit on a stalk. New Zealand podocarps include the totara, kahikatea, rimu, miro and matai.

sauropod – any of a group of plant-eating dinosaurs, typically with pillar-like legs and a long neck and tail.

sedimentary – (of or relating to) rock formed from particles laid down by water.

sinter terrace – rock platform made from minerals that settle out of groundwater.

species – population of individuals that are essentially similar and can breed with one another.

subduction – process by which two **tectonic** plates come together and the heavier plate is forced beneath the other's edge.

supercontinent – very large land mass consisting of several continental land masses. An example of a supercontinent is Pangaea, which broke up into smaller land masses (including the supercontinents Laurasia and Gondwana) in the Mesozoic era.

tectonic plate – any of about 17 plates in Earth's shell that are very slowly moving over the planet's surface.

theropod – member of saurischian ('lizard-hipped') dinosaur group, typically with large, powerful hind limbs and a long tail that stuck straight out behind, balancing the forequarters.

tsunami – pressure wave that very rapidly traverses ocean waters from its point of origin (usually an earthquake), and can cause great damage when it hits coasts.

tuff – rock made from solidified volcanic ash.

vertebrate – animal with a backbone.

zooplankton – collective name for various small animals and their larval forms that populate ocean waters.

BIBLIOGRAPHY

Andrews, Philip, *Tarawera and the Terraces* (2nd edition, revised). Philip Andres: 1995.

Benton, Michael, *Vertebrate Palaeontology* (2nd edition). Oxford: Blackwell Science, 2000.

Campbell, Hamish, and Hutching, Gerard, *In Search of Ancient New Zealand*. Auckland: Penguin Books, 2007.

Cometti, Ronald, *New Zealand's Forest Treasures*. Auckland: Reed, 2002.

Cometti, Ronald, *New Zealand Land of Trees*. Auckland: Reed, 2005.

De Roy, Tui, and Jones, Mark, *New Zealand: A Natural World Revealed*. Auckland: David Bateman, 2006.

Fothergill, Alastair, *Life in the Freezer: A natural history of the Antarctic*. London: BBC Books, 1993.

Gibbs, George, *Ghosts of Gondwana*. Nelson: Craig Potton Publishing, 2006.

Gill, Brian, and Martinson, Paul, *New Zealand's Extinct Birds*. Auckland: Random Century, 1991.

Gill, Brian, and Moon, Geoff, *New Zealand's Unique Birds*. Auckland: Reed, 1999.

Haines, Tim, and Chambers, Paul, *The Complete Guide to Prehistoric Life*. London: BBC Books, 2005.

Keam, Prof. Ronald, *Tarawera*. Auckland: www.tarawera.com, 1988.

Levin, Harold, *The Earth Through Time* (6th edition). Orlando: Saunders College Publishing, 1999.

Metcalf, Lawrie, *Photographic Guide to Alpine Plants of New Zealand*. Auckland: New Holland, 2006.

Molloy, Les, and Cubitt, Gerald, *Wild New Zealand*. London: New Holland Publishers, 1994.

Moon, Lynnette, and Moon, Geoff, *Know Your New Zealand Birds*. Auckland: New Holland, 2006.

Morton, John, and Cometti, Ronald, *Margins of the Sea*. Auckland: Hodder & Stoughton, 1985.

Norman, David, *Prehistoric Life*. New York: Macmillan, 1994.

Parker, Steve, *Dinosaurus: The Complete Guide*. Ontario: Firefly Books, 2003.

Roots, David, Willis, Paul, and Brett-Surman, Michael K. (consultant eds.), *Rocks, Fossils and Dinosaurs*. San Francisco: Fog City Press, 2002.

Stevens, Graeme, McGlone, Matt, and McCulloch, Beverley, *Prehistoric New Zealand*. Auckland: Heinemann Reed, 1988.

Tarbuck, Edward J., and Lutgens, Frederick K., *Earth Science* (10th edition). New Jersey: Pearson Education Inc., 2004.

Tennyson, Alan, and Martinson, Paul, *Extinct Birds of New Zealand*. Wellington: Te Papa Press, 2006.

Wright, Matthew, *Quake*. Auckland: Reed, 2001.

Index